RARE BEAUTY:
Bonita Granville
A BIOGRAPHY

By Kate Arndt

Rare Beauty: Bonita Granville A Biography
By Kate Arndt

Published in the USA by:
BearManor Media
1317 Edgewater Dr #110
Orlando, FL 32804
www.bearmanormedia.com

Perfect ISBN 979-8-88771-745-6
Case ISBN 979-8-88771-746-3
BearManor Media, Orlando, Florida
Printed in the United States of America
Book design by Robbie Adkins, www.adkinsconsult.com

To Linda and Sabrina, your mother and grandma are everything to me and I hope that this book shows you how much I care.

To Bonita, you have saved me more times than you'll ever know.

To the Granville fans, let's do this!

Table of Contents

PART ONE: BONITA

Bonita with actress Anne Shirley at the Hollywood Canteen - 1943, Author's collection

"Nobody's perfect! But Bonita Granville was pretty damn close!"—Gloria Jean (1926-2018).

Prologue: The Glam Girl October 1943

At the Hollywood Canteen stood a woman with blonde hair and stunning blue eyes. She wanted to make sure that everyone was having a good time. This woman was Bonita Granville. The film The Glass Key (1942) had just been released, and she was trying to be taken seriously as an actress. She had been in the business for as long as she could remember.

"Bunny," as she was known to many people, danced and enjoyed her time with the servicemen. Bonita's nature was generous and kind. But to the men, she was considered one of the most beautiful blondes they had ever seen.

She wanted to be seen as a woman, and not as the child star she once was. At 19, she had the world at her fingertips, but she did not know it yet.

That night, she met up with friends Anne Shirley and Deanna Durbin. Bonita knew that Deanna was having marital problems. But Deanna assured her that she was there to have a good time and not to worry about her marriage. Bonita made sure her friend was okay, and then was asked by a soldier to dance. Of course, she said "yes." Why wouldn't she?

Bonita was five-feet tall, and that's all. She was a short but lively woman.

She had about 10 years of show business experience under her belt. The once child star was now a woman—at least to these men—and she was probably one of the younger ones.

Actress Gloria Jean, who saw Bonita that night, said, "Bonita was dressed to the nines, and her eyes sparkled. Considerably, Bonita danced and danced some more, and that wasn't the end of it. She tried not to smoke, but she did."

Underage, she slipped beneath every crack. No one really knew her age, they just assumed she was there to have a good time and she was. She danced and laughed a lot. She always had a smile on her face. According to Gloria Jean, Bonita was perhaps the most vibrant one there that night. Yes, there was Bette Davis, and others, but Bonita was the one who everyone wanted to see. It was then and there Bonita felt more like an adult, rather than a silly child. She wanted to explore this newfound fame she had.

But people didn't realize that Bonita Granville was going to be a big star, in ways that couldn't be imagined on that night in 1942. Bonita's beauty dazzled and she wanted more than ever to be among her peers and help with the war effort.

She talked with Anne Shirley, Gloria Jean, and with soldiers and she was the belle of the place. Bonita's career was flourishing but she didn't realize it at the time. With the war going on, Bonita Granville wanted to present herself as a serious actress and not as the child star that made her a household name. There was so much more to her than Nancy Drew, so much more to her than that.

Baby Bonita in a promo - 1935, (Harry Ransom Center, UT)

Chapter One: Bunny Is Born

In June of 1959, Bonita Granville sat for an interview conducted by Mr. and Mrs. Robert C. Franklin of the Oral Research Office at Columbia University in New York. In some cases, people have thought that Bonita was born in Chicago, but this was an error; as she stated herself, she hailed from New York.

Bonita Gloria Granville arrived on February 2, 1923, in New York, to Bernard "Bunny" Granville and Rosina Timponi, both vaudevillians. Bernard was in the *Ziegfeld Follies.* He was not keen on being a father, as far as Bonita was concerned. She really tried to learn a lot from her father. Bernard was a businessman who took his work seriously.

Bonita stated in an interview, "When talkies came out, my father went to work at Warner Brothers to make three musicals for them and Mommy and I went with him. There was no discussion of me going into pictures at that time."

The marriage between Bernard and Rosina was stormy. As Bonita said, "After Father did the films, he went back to New York and did a radio show. Mother and I stayed in California and we really liked it, so we settled." Bonita's parents split, leaving Bonita without a father. To her, she was too young to understand the situation.

Bonita's charm earned her the acceptance of the neighbors. She and her mother lived in an apartment building where a lot of film stars, producers and show people lived. Bonita and her mother talked with a casting director who resided there. Bonita later explained how she got into the film business, although she never mentioned the casting director's name; however, on IMDB the credit for casting is Charles Richards. Charles told them that RKO had been looking for a little girl to play Ann Harding's daughter in a movie. Bonita said, "He said 20 to 30 girls had already tested for the part and none of them looked like Ann Harding. I had long blonde hair and I looked very much like Ann. I tested with no acting experience whatsoever. I tested and I got it."

It was a part she easily won. Her charm and beauty got her noticed and she was cast in *Westward Passage* (1932), starring Ann Harding and Laurence Olivier. Bonita's part was small, but noticeable. Bonita's mother had to choose between putting her daughter in pictures or finding some other way to pay the bills. The little 9-year-old smiled and was intrigued by the lights and sets. Her heart knew that she had to help support her mother and this was the perfect way to do it.

Bonita's stardom wasn't reached just yet. She slipped into a few roles that were uncredited or too small for her to be noticed. When Bonita was cast in the film *Cavalcade* (1933), she was the only American in the cast. In her 1959 interview, she mentioned that she had taken accent lessons to acquire a "cockney accent." There was only one problem: Bonita doesn't have lines in the movie. She doesn't say a word. She dances, and she prances around, but lines? None. The film won an Oscar for Best Picture.

Bonita's film career was progressing at a gradual pace, but she was on the verge of receiving the most significant role of her life.

Got milk? 1935, (Harry Ransom Center, UT)

Bonita Granville in the early 30's. (Author's personal Collection)

Bonita and Jimmy Durante at the Premiere of Calvacade

"Do you want Pie or not?" Bonita in a promo in 1935 (Harry Ransom Center)

One of her first headshots (Author's Personal Collection)

Bonita in Calvacade *(Author's Personal Collection)*

Bonita, Alma Kruger and Margaret Hamilton in These Three, *1936 (Gift of Jorge Finkelman)*

"You never know with children! But Bonita? How could she be the brat? She was far from one!"— Helen Parrish (1923–1959).

CHAPTER TWO: THE BEGINNING

BONITA STROVE FOR more work, and when the film *These Three* (1936) was being made, she was not the first choice, nor was she even thought of for the part of Mary Tilford, the bratty girl who ruins the lives of her teachers.

Bonita said,

> "*These Three* was really the turning point in my early career. As you know, it was taken from the Lillian Hellman play *The Children's Hour*, which has since been done on Broadway a couple of times, I believe. It starred Merle

Oberon, Joel McCrea and Miriam Hopkins. They had an intensive search for this part, too. I was a little girl with long blonde curls and blue eyes and while I was not very pretty, I was kind of simple and sweet looking, they seemed to think. I was taken up for an interview with the casting director and he turned me down flat.

But they got pretty desperate, and decided they'd interview all of the children, so I went up again to meet Mr. W [William] Wyler and Lillian Hellman. They told me to go away and read the script, and come back to do a reading for them. They were so exhausted with making tests that they didn't want to take another test until they'd first had a reading.

So, I came back the next day, with my little part all read. My mother helped me tremendously with this particular thing, because we'd worked very hard on it. By this time, I think I was eleven or twelve, and I knew how to work a little bit.

I studied and decided I could go in and read for them and I did. All they said to me was, "We'd like to take you up to meet Mr. Samuel Goldwyn." Of course, by this time I couldn't even talk. My knees were shaking. We went up to see Mr. Goldwyn. He was terribly polite, and I read to him. Mr. Goldwyn didn't say a word to me, not one word. I thought: "Well, maybe I'm going to get a test." I knew if they didn't like the reading they wouldn't spend any more money on tests.

He said, "Little girl, will you go over in the corner and let me talk about you?" I did and they did. I don't remember how long they spent—it seemed like an eternity to me, but I'm sure it wasn't more than ten or fifteen minutes—and I went over, sitting in the same room where they conferred, which was a tremendous office. He called me back and said, "Would you like to play this part?" I said, "Oh, very much, Mr. Goldwyn. Do you suppose I could

> take the test?" He said, "No, you can't take a test. The part is yours."

Bonita's excitement had to be concealed, but she was thrilled. The part of Mary Tilford was the part that she'd be most remembered for. Bonita, who was gentle and kind, had to do something she was not used to at all: Be mean and bratty.

Bonita had called *These Three* a picture she didn't necessarily regret, but she didn't want to be seen as that character. The studio dyed her hair almost black, which really upset Bonita. They did this to make her look meaner. It worked, and Bonita's performance is one that audiences never forgot.

When the film was released on March 18, 1936, Bonita's performance was praised, but had parents in an uproar. Bonita, being a kind-spirited girl, wasn't exactly sure why mothers were writing her letters explicitly telling her she had "better straighten up or else!"

"I would receive Bibles," she recalled. Mothers in churches would see the film and thought Bonita was that ghastly.

"*These Three* was an inaccurate representation of Bonita," actress Marcia Mae Jones said. Jones played Rosalie in the film and shared the majority of the scenes with Granville. They hit it off, and as Marcia recalled, "She knew how to turn on that mean charm, but when the cameras stopped rolling, she would be so apologetic."

Bonita's interviews at the time of the film's release consistently urged the audience not to perceive her as a mean, spoiled brat, as she was nothing like that character. She was so good in *These Three* she was nominated for an Oscar as Best Actress in a Supporting Role, but sadly, she lost to Gale Sondergaard (*Anthony Adverse*).

When she went back to school at LeConte Junior High School, Bonita sometimes acted a little too big for her britches. As iconic Tap Dancer and Actress, Ann Miller recalled in her book, *Miller's High Life:*

> "I had enrolled in LeConte Junior High School. I remember it mainly because that is where I met Bonita Granville. She was very big as a child star at the time. She had just finished a picture called These Three, in which she played the role of a mean little brat. She was

a tremendous hit in this film and a big celebrity in my school. In other words, she was a Big Shot and the center of attention because she was a Big Movie Star. I secretly admired her very much.

I was Captain of the Commissary at my school, which meant that it was my job to help patrol the commissary and see that only those children who bought and paid for their own hot lunches had seats inside. Children who brought their lunches from home were not permitted to sit inside the commissary because there were only enough chairs and tables for the children who were paying for their lunches. There were tables outside for the lunch-bringers, and my orders as Captain of the Commissary were not to let any child come in with a lunch brought from home.

Well, Miss Big Shot Bonita used to bring her lunch from home and sneak into the commissary with her chums and sit there and eat with them while they were eating their hot lunches.

I went over to her one day and said, "I'm sorry, Bonita, but you can't stay in here." I explained to her that she was taking up a seat that rightfully belonged to someone else who had bought a hot lunch in the commissary. She told me she was almost finished. She just sat there and laughed and then she walked out with her chums.

We went through this routine twice. The third time she got snippety with me and snapped, "I'm going to sit here whether you like it or not."

I was so angry I couldn't control my Aries temper so I just hauled off and slapped her, and we had a terrible cat-and-dog fight right there. The teachers broke us up and we were both taken into the principal's office and reprimanded and sent home from school. The principal said I was right in trying to keep her out of the commissary but

> that I should not have slapped her. That temper of mine was bad.
>
> We're good friends today and Bonita and I reminisce and laugh about it quite often. We have something else in common also. We like oil men. Bonita is now married to a very wealthy and handsome oil man from Texas, Jack Wrather. She obviously has had better luck with her oil man than I had with my three.
>
> They own several television stations, and Bonita is also a successful TV producer. She produces the Lassie show."

During her time with Samuel Goldwyn, she made a concerted effort to maintain a high level of professionalism, all while navigating the challenges of being a pre-teen. The world around her was getting bigger and she wanted to do bigger and better pictures.

Bonita's first Warner Brother's headshot (Author's collection)

"There's always a right or wrong, but when it came to Bonita, she was usually right!"—Jackie Moran (1923-1990).

Chapter Three: Bonita the "Brat"

Bonita's career was not at a standstill, and ahe began her next picture, *Maid of Salem* (1937), directed by Frank Lloyd. When it came to playing brats, Bonita was the top person to do it. This time, she played Ann Williams of Salem, who pretends to be bewitched—and again caused chaos for a little Puritan town. Before *The Crucible,* this was it.

The film was made by Paramount Pictures, a studio that she would come to know well in the future. She was loaned from Samuel Goldwyn to Paramount to make the picture and from all accounts, Bonita had taken full advantage of her dramatic role—she screamed and she flung about. The film starred Claudette Colbert, Fred MacMurray and Virginia Weidler.

The film got Bonita noticed by Warner Brothers, who offered the fourteen-year-old a contract of $500 a week, which in those days paid thc bills. Bonita took it. They immediately cast her opposite Olivia de Havilland in *Call It a Day* (1937), a film really centered around de Havilland. But, unlike other studios, Warner Brothers knew what to do with their pint-size prodigy. They saw that they had a rare talent on their hands with Bonita and they decided to make use of her.

Bonita's next project was the highly anticipated *The Beloved Brat* (1938), which starred Dolores Costello. Bonita played Roberta Morgan whose wealthy parents gave her plenty of material possessions but who basically ignored her. She acts out and torments the family butler Jenkins. The only person to take notice of her thirteenth birthday is her father's secretary, Williams. She makes friends with a black boy, Pinkie White (Matthew "Stymie" Beard), and visits his home. She is impressed by the love Pinkie's mother, Mrs. White, shows Pinkie and his sister Arabella.

Roberta invites Pinkie to dinner and Jenkins angrily throws him out. When her parents go away, her misbehavior escalates, and Jenkins locks her in her room. She sets fire to it and escapes. Jenkins tracks her to Pinkie's house. On the way home in the car, they argue. Roberta grabs the steering wheel, resulting in the vehicle veering into the path of an oncoming car and to the driver's death. Roberta tells the police that Jenkins was drinking and the butler is sentenced to prison for manslaughter.

Guilt-ridden, she confesses that she made it up. Roberta is sentenced to a special girls' school run by Helen Cosgrove (played by Dolores Costello). Helen manages to reform Roberta by getting her to help the younger students. When Roberta is allowed to return home, she refuses to leave. Her parents hear about this and change their ways.

Bonita's hesitation to take this picture stemmed from her apprehension about the feedback she received during the filming of *These Three*. But, really, the film did just the opposite. In *These Three,* Bonita was a brat throughout the film; in this, her battiness evolves throughout the film, ultimately transforming her into a charming character. You feel sorry for Bonita's character, as she's neglected. A spoiled child, she had everything she could ever want, except one thing: Parents who loved her.

Bonita felt she couldn't relate to Roberta, but her fears were alleviated when the critics praised her performance. In time, *The Beloved Brat* became a classic. The film itself is heartwarming, but not without a rocky beginning, for the film, again, tainted Bonita as a "brat." Bonita's fears about her being typecasted as a brat seemed to overwhelm her. Luckily, for her, that anxious feeling would be alleviated.

Bonita's mother made sure that she had as normal a life as possible. She was able to make friends with other child stars and some of those child stars included Anne Shirley (1918-1993), Deanna Durbin (1921-2013), Helen Parrish (1923-1959), Judy Garland (1922-1969), Jackie Cooper (1922-2011), Gloria Jean (1926-

2018), and one of her dearest friends, Ann Rutherford (1917-2012). She went to their homes, went to parties with them, as well as on dates.

Bonita was no stranger to the publicity department taking photos of her every move. She was a child star, now growing up. When she began her period when she was 15, she tried to contain her pain by telling Helen Parrish that she was "a woman now." The 15-year-old couldn't

Helen and Bonita had a bond that no one could ever break. Helen was a child star at Universal. In 1938, when they met at a gathering, Bonita had just completed *Call It a Day* and Helen had just completed the Durbin picture *Mad About Music*. Bonita, Helen and Deanna met each other around the same time. In an interview Helen did in the early '50s, she said, "Bonita's magnetic personality drew me to her. She was a cheerful and lovely woman, who really loved to laugh and she was very funny. She was a dear friend, who listened and was a friend who really gave a shit about you. She put you first and she was encouraging, and lovely in every way."

With Bonita making friends everywhere she went, she really became the girl next door, the girl that you wanted to bring home to your mother and your father. Bonita, was a "good girl," always had manners and was always pleasant. But that didn't mean, she didn't have a playfulness about her as well. She would run with the other girls in the neighborhood and have a grand ol'e time.

Helen's friendship with Bonita really blossomed in 1939, when Bonita was working on a Nancy Drew movie. Bonita's kindness definitely got the shy Helen out of her shell. Bonita would be considered an extrovert, while Helen had her reservations about Hollywood.

Something that a lot of people wouldn't know about Helen Parrish, is that she had been catapulted into showbusiness by her mother. Unlike Bonita's mother, who raised her daughter with love and care, Helen's mother was a little different. Helen had an older sister named Beverly. She was a struggling child actress who only had one credit to her name. Beverly and Helen were not seen as children but as cash cows to their mother. She was a stage mother and wanted nothing more than for her children to be famous. Beverly and Helen were placed in the spotlight when they were able to walk and talk. Helen first started when she was 5 months old and Beverly started when she was two. Beverly did not make it far in Hollywood.

Beverly suddenly died on February 27, 1930 at the age of 11. This began Helen's hell with her mother. Helen managed to get roles in feature films but was never a leading lady. Her mother made comments to her like "Beverly would have acted circles around you!" This began Helen's 'survivor guilt' that she would feel for the rest of her life.

Bonita did not know Beverly. Sometimes Bonita would hear such comments from Helen's mother, and would be sad for her friend. Bonita would ask her friend, *"Why would your mother say such things about you? And... Whose Beverly?"* Helen had to quickly explain that she had a sister who died. Bonita said,

"That's not an excuse for your mother to say such things about you. You're a wonderful actress and you're just as good as everyone else!" Bonita was correct, Helen Parrish was a terrific actress, but was never really appreciated, unless it was by the great friends that she knew, which included a roster of women, such as: Deanna Durbin, Gloria Jean, Peggy Moran (Koster), Anne Shirley, Judy Garland and of course, Bonita Granville.

With Bonita being at Warner's, her next assignment would indeed change her life. What Bonita didn't know, is how much it would change her life, and make her an icon, for one very special role.

A publicity portrait of Bonita at Warner Brothers (Author's collection)

A publicity of Bonita in My Bill (Author's collection)

Bonita's first publicity at MGM (Author's Collection)

Bonita with her mother (Author's collection)

Bonita at Warner Brothers, 1939, (Author's Collection)

Bonita at Warner Brothers (Harry Ransom Center, UT)

Bonita promoting education for Warner Brothers (Harry Ransom Center, UT)

Publicity from The Beloved Brat
(Harry Ransom Center, UT)

More publicity from The Beloved Brat *(Harry Ransom Center, UT)*

Bonita's publicity headshot for Warner Brothers
(Author's collection)

Bonita at her time at Warner Brothers (Author's collection)

Bonita in a publicity for Nancy Drew Detective *(Gift of Jorge Finkelman)*

"The time of her life was working as Nancy Drew. She became an ICON"—Frankie Thomas (1921-2006)

CHAPTER FOUR: NANCY DREW

BONITA ALWAYS SAID she was lucky, and in 1938 that luck would come in handy. "Most of my success I had up until that point was *luck*! I was indeed a very lucky little girl!"

In 1938, Jack Warner aimed to compete with MGM's *Andy Hardy* series, and the project he sought to develop was the Nancy Drew stories authored by Carolyn Keene (a pseudonym for various writers). The first book they adapted was *The Password to Larkspur Lane*. This time, Bonita was the first pick for the role. She earned this and she really tried to make it worthwhile.

"I was growing up, starting the teenage thing—driving a car," she said. "I wasn't really old enough to drive a car. They taught me to drive a car in this series. The Nancy Drew series was a great maturing kind of thing for me personally."

Bonita did more than just learn to drive a car; she learned how to be a young teenager. She learned how to dress more maturely and she learned how to be a young lady. She said that this role made her learn to be herself, which to her, was the hardest thing she ever had to do.

She later said, "Just playing myself was kind of my problem. As a matter of fact, it's always been one of my problems." Bonita was like any girl at that age, dealing with boy problems, self-esteem issues and the fact that she did her growing up in front of the public.

Bonita's first Nancy Drew film was *Nancy Drew: Detective* (1938). The film co-starred veteran child actor Frankie Thomas. Frankie had been in the business since he was young, now he was turning 18, practically an adult. Bonita, being only 16, seemed so inexperienced to take on this role. But to William Clemens, the director, Bonita was perfect. She did have reservations about playing such an iconic character. "She was something that I felt a lot of pressure playing. I was ready, but at the same time, I felt that I wasn't ready."

Frankie Thomas was no stranger to being in the limelight. Being a few years older than Bonita made him have a sense of protection over her. Bonita was already trying to get through the day by being herself, and with that, came her personality. "I found her to be a gentle person. Her spirituality was incredible and she took her job seriously," Frankie said. Bonita's attachment to Frankie would last their entire lives.

Frankie's acting career began in 1934, around the same time Bonita began her career. Bonita felt Thomas to be a boy she could converse with and she seemed to get on well with him. Though people tried to make them a romantic couple, Thomas would deny any type of sexual attraction to his co-star.

He said, "Though I found her beautiful, I found her to be more of a friend than anything and if I had to kiss her, I would, but not unless I had to." Frankie and Bonita would be paired in five pictures together: *Nancy Drew: Detective* (1938), *Angels Wash Their Faces* (1939), *Nancy Drew... Reporter* (1939), *Nancy Drew and the Hidden Staircase* (1939) and *Nancy Drew... Trouble Shooter* (1939). Frankie and Bonita shared more than the screen together, they shared their lives and mutual friends. Some of their mutual friends were Helen Parrish, Deanna Durbin, Freddie Bartholomew, Jackie Cooper, Jackie Searl and Judy Garland. The interesting part about them sharing mutual friends, is that they all "worked" in the same circles. This meant that a lot of them had worked together before. Bonita, being part of the once Golden Age studio system, worked with Thomas a lot, because they were both under contract to Warner Brothers.

The Nancy Drew series proved to be a big success at Warner Brothers, so much so that they capitalized on Bonita's success. Bonita wanted to please her audience. With Bonita's success, she found it more compelling to be the good girl, and she was eager to please. "Bonita's personality really came out when we were shooting *Nancy Drew: Reporter*," Thomas later said.

Bonita understood what it meant to grow up in the public eye. "All my 'dates' were set up by different studios and we were all thrown together," Bonita said. It was the main reason that people would see Bonita on different lots or with different child stars, some she had never met before, until that moment of the shoot.

Bonita's personality usually glowed, and with other stars, they usually liked her, but sometimes, they would find her too nice, which again never made much sense. Bonita's kind spirit would sometimes be overlooked as fake, but there was nothing fake about her. Her charm was real. As Linda Darnell once said about Bonita,

"That little girl was a charmer, but she had a real swell heart that never broke." In other words, Linda always said Bonita as a kind woman, who had a great big heart, but little did she know, Bonita's heart did break, more than once, but with her professionalism, she never showed it.

Other starlets were trying to figure out their place in Hollywood, Bonita was no different.

"When I did Nancy Drew, I was still learning how to be an all-American girl, and yet trying to be a woman," Bonita would later say. Bonita's role as Nancy Drew would become her greatest one to date, and one she would be remembered for.

With the role of Nancy Drew being such a big staple in the 1930s, Bonita's fame began to shoot up. She wasn't Bette Davis, but she was getting recognition. She was interviewed and she was gaining popularity among the young girls in the United States. With that being said, Bonita's own changes were drastic, and normal. She stopped growing, but she said, "I'm growing in other places too."

Bonita's approach to each role was a challenge. In *Nancy Drew... Reporter*, she got to do a musical number, which she loved. She was not dubbed and she was excited to be able to show off her natural singing ability.

In *Nancy Drew... Trouble Shooter*, she had to learn about aviation. She was thrilled about learning new things, and in *Nancy Drew: Detective* she learned about pigeons and Morse code.

The publicity from the films helped her to accept the things she could not confirm nor deny.

According to the publicity, she was in bed by 11:00 p.m., but, really, she was in bed by 10:00 p.m., or earlier. These rumors made it seem she was a night owl and it was always baffling to her. "I believe I am the one who people want to make out to be a person that I'm not," she once said.

It was also claimed that she got to pick out her own clothes for the film. As it said in the pressbook for *Nancy Drew... Reporter*:

> "Because Milo Anderson believes sixteen-year-old girls should have a hand in selecting their own clothes, he took Bonita Granville, the star of *Nancy Drew—Reporter*, the Warner Bros. picture opening Friday at the Strand Theatre, into his confidence when he planned her wardrobe for the picture. The result was three charming sports ensembles—all done up in poudre blue. That happened to be Bonita's favorite color and Milo carried out her preference because the color had splendid photographic properties, showing up as a smooth, rich gray on the screen.
>
> In one outfit, Milo combines a poudre blue angora sweater and matching felt hat with a smoky blue flannel skirt and a short boxy jacket of oyster white plaited in shades of light blue.
>
> For another costume, designer and star agreed upon a short basque jacket of Roseberry wool crepe fastened snugly down the front with self-covered little buttons and briefly caped. In this case, the Peter Pan collar, the lining of the cape, the flared wool crepe skirt, felt hat and stitched suede gloves are all of poudre blue. Bonita teams these same accessories with another ensemble, which consists of a butterfly pleated red, white and blue plaid wool skirt, light poudre blue blouse and belt and deep poudre Eton jacket of wool crepe. Milo Anderson and Bonita became great friends during their working hours and Milo, apparently serious, offered her a job in his department whenever she wanted one."

Bonita's opinions sometimes rarely mattered. However, when there was publicity about her, she took it.

With Bonita being Nancy Drew, there was more publicity, including one that she got a "kiss" for her 16th birthday.

> **"GETS A KISS FOR 16th BIRTHDAY**
>
> Celebration of, her sixteenth birthday recently held unusual significance for Bonita Granville.
>
> In honor of her natal day her mother, Mrs. Bernard Granville, officially sanctioned screen kisses for her for the first time. And that day, for the first time, Bonita received a screen kiss.
>
> The fact that it was her birthday did not mean that the lovely little Warner Bros. starlet was to have a holiday from screen work. As a matter of fact it was the starting day for her latest picture, "Naney Drew—Troubleshooter," which opens next Friday at the Strand Theatre.
>
> The ban on kissing having been lifted, Director William Clemens thought it fitting and proper that the first screen to be filmed on her birthday should be the one in which Bonita's leading man, 17-year-old Frankie Thomas, would kiss her.
>
> The sixteenth birthday kiss met entirely with Bonita's approval.
>
> "I wouldn't want to be known as sweet sixteen and never been kissed," she said.
>
> There was a certain diffidence on the part of the participants as the scene was rehearsed. Bonita preserved a degree of womanly composure but Frankie fidgeted with collar and seemed to possess a rosier complexion than usual. The scene was completed to the complete satisfaction of all concerned, however. Another milestone had been passed in the careers of two up-and coming movie stars.

Naturally, members of the cast and technical crew couldn't resist a little teasing. After all, they've gotten to be more or less like a family group, since the filming of the popular series brings them together so frequently, and like all family groups they're given to teasing the younger members. The youngsters, however, refused to be rattled.

"It's kind of silly — but nice, don't you think?" was Bonita's only comment.

Other indications of Bonita's official "growing-up" were that at her birthday party that night, she wore a long dress, and had her curls pinned high on her head. But, lest there be some who hate to see their favorite young starlet turning into an adult so quickly, let it be said that the next day, back at work on her latest "Naney Drew" adventure, Bonita seemed to have forgotten all about being grown up. She and Frankie were back on the old, teasing friendship basis, and lunchtime found her more than ready for the midday nap routine she has followed ever since she started working in pictures. Which proves that the growing up process is a long one."

Another publicity was all about "Tips for Teens"

"TIPS FOR THE 'TEENS'

Considering that Bonita Granville sets fashions for the Hollywood High School crowd, cork will doubtless soon be its pet sports jewelry, for Bonita has been playing tennis in a white pique play suit accented by a necklace of vari-colored cork balls, pastel and perfumed.

Bonita Granville wasn't allowed to go horseback riding while "Nancy Drew—Trouble Shooter," was in production, so she organized the "Teeners" (formerly the "Twelvers") into a bicycle brigade. Her newest riding rompers are featherweight rose suede and with them she wears a quilted green suede jacket and beret.

The 16-year-old plotting a summer travelling ensemble would do well to consider the suit Milo Anderson designed for Bonita Granville to wear in "Nancy Drew—Trouble Shooter." It is of grey wool fabric resembling Kasha-clothes. The skirt is fashioned with all-round pleats stitched down to lower hipline, while the square-shouldered boxy jacket is collarless and loose.

Bonita Granville, one of whose hobbies is collecting candy recipes, has received them from girls all over the world, but her favorite is still this recipe for "fool-proof" fudge: In a saucepan combine 2 cups sugar, 2/3 cup canned evaporated milk, and 2 heaping tablespoonsful cocoa. Boil it slowly with a minimum of stirring until it forms a soft ball in cold water. Take off fire, add 1 teaspoon butter and 1/2 teaspoon vanilla, allow it to cool for a few minutes, then set saucepan in shallow pan of cold water. Beat fudge until creamy, then turn it into buttered tin and chill.

Although Bonita Granville, now 16, is not permitted to use high-colored nail polish, she has other definite ideas about youthful hand beauty. She washes her hands many times a day but never goes outside without drying them thoroughly and softening them with hand cream. Sometimes she combines a beauty treatment with her evening study hour, dipping her fingers in hot castor oil and wearing cotton gloves while she reads."

The Magazine articles covering the series were just as interesting, making Bonita seem like she had it "all together."

"Bonita A Miss Now

Bonita Granville celebrated her sixteenth birthday the way every girl in the world would like to, In the morning she began her third starring role in "Nancy Drew—Trouble Shooter," and in the evening she donned her first floor-length evening dress and, in the best sixteen-year-old tradition pinned her curls high on her head."

When *Nancy Drew Reporter* came out, the publicity continued! It got even bigger than the first one.

> **"Bonita Granville Experts' Choice As Nancy Drew**
>
> Bonita Granville is Hollywood's choice as the typical sixteen year-old American girl, At least she was chosen by the Warner Bros. Studio to play the role of Nancy Drew in the series of pictures being made from the novels written about that remarkable young lady in the past thirty years and popular with juveniles and adolescents through all those years.
>
> Bonita became sixteen herself in February, and she is a completely normal, healthy girl who is average in her school work, pretty in a youthful way and no better and no worse in her average behavior than any other girl her age.
>
> Emily Post and Kathleen Norris, among others, helped to supply the information the studio used in selecting Bonita for the Nancy Drew roles. These authorities described Miss Sweet Sixteen as a girl who doesn't smoke or drink, has boyfriends but no "steady," stays out until eleven o'clock at night and has not yet learned to cook or keep house.
>
> Bonita's own answers to the same set of questions matched the guesses of the older women quite closely. She doesn't smoke or drink, is not allowed to stay out at night unchaperoned, has an allowance of spending money, helps her mother buy her clothes and is a "tomboy" by day and a "lady" by night. She "hates housework" and can't cook.
>
> She brought a supply of high school slanguage to the first picture of the series with her and the script was modified to include some of it.
>
> Producer and Director were interested. They took Bonita and Frankie Thomas, who plays opposite her, into a story conference and recorded their suggestions of dialogue changes, Naturally, the lesson thus learned was applied

> to the script of the second picture of the series, "Nancy Drew—Reporter," which opens next Friday at the Strand Theatre. Bonita lives with her mother in a Hollywood apartment. Between pictures she attends Hollywood High School and when she is working, she has a special teacher on the set to keep her even with her classes. She likes to dance, swim and ride horseback."

In this publicity article, there were a few things that were true about it.

First, Bonita couldn't cook, her daughter, Linda, could confirm that. Also, she did share an apartment with her mother, however, in 1940, she was able to buy her first of many homes. With Bonita's education, she did however go to Hollywood High, only to really try to "maintain a normal life" as much as possible. Bonita did everything she could to fit in, and she succeeded, but unlike most of her peers, she had a full-time job. A job, in the picture industry. She did get a high school degree, and that she always said, "Was one of my biggest achievements."

Another thing that the article did get right about Bonita, is that she did love swimming and she loved to dance, but not so much of horseback riding. But, she did love animals, of all kinds.

In the book *Hollywood Kids* by Thomas G Aylesworth, he stated this about Bonita in *Nancy Drew* .

> *"One of the roles for which Granville is best remembered is that of Nancy Drew, the teenage girl detective in the series that Warner Bros. hoped would compete with the Andy Hardy films. Nancy's attorney father (John Litel) let her come and go as she pleased. Her boy friend, Ted Nickerson (he was Ned Nickerson in the books on which the films were based), was played by Frankie Thomas, who had been the star of A Dog of Flanders (1935) and the serial Tim Tyler's Luck (1937), based on the comic strip by Lyman Young.*
>
> *Nancy Drew-Detective (1938) was the first of the series; it centered on the disappearance of an elderly lady who had promised her school a large endowment. In 1939 came such*

> *bits of fluff as Nancy Drew–Reporter, which also featured Dickie Moore;*
>
> *Nancy Drew–Trouble Shooter, and Nancy Drew and the Hidden Staircase, the best of the lot. The Nancy Drew series collapsed after Hidden Staircase. The problem was that Nancy Drew wasn't really old enough to be kissed by boys, much less, like Andy Hardy, to have innumerable romantic problems."*

Bonita's publicity for the film, also made the announcement that she turned sweet sixteen!

> **"Bonita Is Sixteen**
>
> Bonita Granville, featured in Warner Bros.' "Nancy Drew— Reporter," which opens next Friday at the Strand Theatre, was born in New York City, Feb. 2, 1923. She went on the stage at the age of three and a half years."
>
> Bonita Granville chose to keep her real age, unlike a lot of her counterparts, their ages were "faked."
>
> Translation: Bonita Granville was really sixteen when she made the film. Her contemporaries, such as Deanna Durbin (1921-2013), had to fake her age. Universal, made her a year younger, than what she was. The studio marked her birth year as 1922, whereas Bonita, said "Nope! I'm keeping my age!"

With Bonita being the "All-American Teenager," she really felt like a girl who was trying to just survive each day. The days at Warner Brothers were quite long. Bonita swiftly acquired the ability to build her stamina over the course of the days that she filming for long periods of time.

Bonita's lasting legacy will have her emulate Nancy Drew. It would take Bonita over 20 years to realize that she made a lasting impact playing Nancy Drew. Even today, she is mentioned when the mediocre and terrible remakes are made. She is the first one that the newspapers always mention because, her Nancy Drew, was the best one and so many people would agree with that sentiment. Bonita's Nancy Drew films still exist, all four of them. Sadly, they have not been made it to the criterion collection yet, but hopefully that will be a reality at some point. It has been remastered several times over the course of 50 years, but it's hard for people who are just discovering these films, that they were made "so long ago." The films themselves are over 80 years old, and that's hard to imagine and yet, they don't look like they've aged at all. That's what makes Bonita's version classics, they're timeless and will never fade out of view. So many young people, including young women, who are introduced to Nancy Drew, soon find themselves in front of a screen watching Bonita Granville solve a mystery and then, they usually want to watch more of this woman, and know how much of an impact she's made for the story of Nancy Drew.

She will always be Nancy Drew, not anyone else could compare and there's no argument there. She is and will always be *Nancy Drew.*

Nancy Drew photoshoot (Harry Ransom Center, UT)

Nancy Drew photoshoot (Harry Ransom Center, UT)

Nancy Drew publicity (Author's collection)

Nancy Drew tests and publicity (Harry Ransom UT)

Bonita with Frankie Thomas (Harry Ransom Center, UT)

Warner Brothers 1939 (Author's Collection)

Bonita posing for a fashion publicity for MGM , 1940 (Author's Collection)

Bonita in an advert (Author's personal Collection)

Bonita promoting jewelry (Author's Collection)

PART TWO: BUNNY

Bonita with Bob Hope, Ann Rutherford, Judy Garland, and Ann Gills (Author's Collection)

"

She was something of a safe space for people! So calm, collected and above all, safe!"—Jane Withers (1926-2021).

CHAPTER FIVE: SAFE ZONE!

"Deanna [Durbin] hates this!" Helen Parrish wrote to Bonita in June of 1941. Deanna Durbin was having marital issues in 1941, and of course, working in the same circles as Helen and Deanna, she knew about as it as well.

In 1941, Bonita's personal life began to spring up like a wildflower. But with that came the saving grace of Bunny Granville.

Bonita loved her life, skillfully navigating her dating life, which, in truth, were not genuine dates but rather orchestrated by the studio. In 1941, Bonita was with MGM. She wasn't screwed over, but men greatly tried her patience. In an email, Gloria Jean had recounted a lunch out with Bonita Granville, Helen Parrish and Jane Withers.

"Jane looked at Bunny with fascination. Jane asked Bunny what was wrong, and Bunny, per usual, told us that nothing was wrong. Now, I knew Jane, she wasn't going to let this go. She asked Bunny again. Of course, I chimed in and asked whose ass am I kicking. Bunny looked at all of us, and told us that there is a man at MGM that will not leave her alone! Of course, I thought, a producer, and she told us it was some assistant man, that she had never seen before. She was getting nervous. Jane told her that we knew, and we did, knew some guys that could talk to him (meaning they'd probably beat him up or threaten his life, you know those kinds of things!). Bunny said that was not necessary, that she'd have to handle it on her own. Helen looked at her in shock and said to her, you don't want to get yourself hurt in the process. Well, a few weeks later, we all met again and this time, Bunny had some shocking news, that the man was just gone, wasn't bothering her anymore! Apparently, what we found out, was that Jane had mentioned it to our good friend, Robert Stack and he had done some talking to this guy, well, low and behold, the guy left her alone! Ah! Thank God for the good men in Hollywood, because not all of them, as you were good. But, if you had good gal pals, like we did, we're there for each other." They were all there for each other, in one way or another and Bonita was different. She was there for her pals, whenever they needed her help. It appears that sometimes, the way that they were needed, Bonita always seemed to be there, right on time.

"Bonita's timing was always ..well on time!" Cora Sue Collins said.

"Bonita would rush over where she needed to be and there she was, helping you out, like she was a saint or an angel. I believe she was both," Cora Sue Collins added. The thing about Bonita Granville was, is that she put other's people's needs before her own, if that person didn't deserve it.

"Her heart was as good as gold and she had it torn by people, who really didn't deserve it! My god that Jackie {Cooper} broke her heart and that shattered her, but she still remained just as cheerful and lovely as ever," Her friend, Ann Rutherford said in an interview about Bonita. She was a survivor, and yet, she loved people with her all her heart and her might. Sometimes, she knew that people who weren't deserving of her affections, she gave it to them anyways.

She always said this about people:

> "If you have a problem with me, talk to me about it. Be a man or a woman and discuss it with me. I don't want to hear it from a third party, because if I do, you don't know me well enough to have a problem with me." This meant, that if there were people who didn't deserve her affections and still talked bad about her, she wanted to hear from your mouth, not from the press, which tragically, was how a lot of the "feuds" or "scandals" got in the way. Luckily

for Bonita, she didn't have to deal with scandals nor have to deal with "bad press."

She had this to say in 1964:

> "When I listened to people talk about me, that I've heard from other people, I ask them why are they relaying this information to me? They usually say, 'Bunny, don't you want to know what so and so said about you?' My answer is this: Why have you picked up the knife and stabbed me with it? They are usually are surprised by my answer. Yes, you've picked up that knife and you've stabbed me with it." Bonita's kindness sometimes was taken for weakness, and as she, figured, it was not something she took lightly. She wanted to be taken seriously, but even she knew her limits.

Another situation that Bonita found herself in, saved one of her friend's lives. In 1944, Bonita's quick thinking saved her friend Deanna Durbin. In tears, Deanna had called Bonita, and Bonita sensed quickly that something was clearly wrong. She asked Deanna, "Where are you?" Deanna told her, and Bonita was quickly on her way. In the car, Bonita prayed to God that Deanna was safe. Bonita managed to find Deanna, on the ledge of a bridge, outside of Los Angeles.

Bonita parked her car and managed to walk slowly to Deanna. She thought that if someone was going to kill themselves, and you wanted to talk them out of it, you had to do it slowly.

"She was just there, crying her little eyes out!" Bonita wrote to Helen Parrish. Bonita's empathetic nature really kicked in and she did everything she could to try to deescalate the situation.

Bonita called out to Deanna. Deanna started crying, cursing Bonita as she did. As Gloria said,

> "Bonita's understanding of suicide was very apparent. I don't know if she ever knew anyone [up to that point] who had died by suicide, but I think her empathetic nature kicked in."

Bonita walked slowly up to Deanna and calmed her down, and as Gloria told it, "Not with Bible verses, but with endearing words of love and appreciation."

Bonita's love reached Durbin in a different manner, from how most individuals might have approached that situation. "Deanna, in about 10 years, you'll be able to walk away, but you cannot do that now, until you realize it's time," Bonita said. In time, Deanna Durbin remembered Bonita's words and, eight years later, Deanna did walk away from Hollywood and never looked back.

Bonita's gentleness tended to save countless lives in Hollywood. But with Durbin, she felt that Deanna needed extra love.

"Bonita's gentle heart made her an easy target to get walked on," Gloria Jean said later. Bonita lent her "healing" hand to her friend, Judy Garland. During the period when Judy was undergoing an abortion, Bonita's compassion and gentle demeanor provided her friend with comfort and affection. With Bonita's beliefs as a Catholic on abortion, she put those aside and took care of Judy, who in her eyes, needed all the love she could offer.

"She never for a moment let anyone feel sorry for her. She always said she had plenty of fun!" Gloria Jean said. Bonita's charm never faded. She always seemed to be the first one to take care of someone, but about herself? She did take care of herself, but she did on her own terms.

"She always was the 'mother' friend of the group," Gloria Jean recalled in a phone conversation in 2015. Bonita felt like a mother to a lot of these women, who she considered friends, even though, many of them were her age, younger or older. Bonita's "motherly" instinct just came naturally to her, and she didn't have children then. She put others before herself, and that was a quality that a lot of her peers, such as Jane Withers or Ann Rutherford, always remembered.

Bonita's mother raised her, and Bonita seemed to inherit the caring and loving personality that her mother had. The beautiful woman endured so much heartbreak and torment at the hands of actresses, who thought they were bigger than life, when in reality, they would be the ones that fell off the rail when their careers were said and done. Bonita, as a lot of her peers noticed, very rarely got sad, and as she said to Gloria Jean in the 1950s, and repeated in her 1959 interview, "When I am sad, I'll go outside and look up at the sky. Have you ever looked at the night sky? Literally look at it and see the stars, aren't they amazing? Can you believe that there is a world beyond ours? That's what I think about when I'm sad, as to how much God has created and yet we don't even take the time to notice it. When I am sad and alone, I think of all the amazing things that He has created, including the night sky, because it is just one way of knowing that we are alive, and that tomorrow, even though it is not promised to us, we can always look up at the sky and know that tomorrow will always be here and I always think to myself the sadness will be temporary, but the sky will always remain and the night sky will always be beautiful." She tried to think of that whenever she felt upset or alone, is that God created this world, and there's so much that she wanted to explore of it. She was always mesmerized by the fact that God, in her mind, had made the mountains and the stars, and how could all this beauty in the world, be taken for granted, by her feeling sorry for herself?

"Ach! There's no time for that! Feeling sorry for oneself!" She always said to her friends.

Bonita's love for others led her to ponder the reasons behind her consistent behavior. Being an empath, Bonita always seemed to empathize with her peers. Bonita's quick thinking was able to shield Deanna from the newspapers when Deanna had a panic attack. Gloria Jean had recounted this story in an email in 2015.

According to Gloria Jean, "I had brought Durbin to Bunny's house. Helen Parrish was already at there. Durbin was having a panic attack and I think a lot of knew why. Bunny was kind and let Durbin use her bathroom for a bath. When she came out, Bunny handed Durbin a velvet blue robe and Durbin put it on. Within minutes, Durbin started screaming bloody murder. Helen ran to Bunny's phone and Bunny screamed, "No! Stop! We will not be having photographers at this house tonight!" I asked what we were going to do. Bunny took a deep breath and she said that she knew that this wasn't right, but there was a bottle of whiskey underneath the kitchen sink. Helen went and got it. She came back and Helen asked what we were going to do with the bottle. Bunny had said that we were going to get Durbin drunk and that was the only way we could think to calm her down. Well, funny enough, it worked, and believe me, it was not easy trying to get this bottle into Durbin's mouth, but we did it." For Deanna, she had a terrible hangover the next day, but Bonita knew how to cure that too: with raw eggs and tobacco sauce. She always said, "Don't ask me how I knew this, I just knew."

Bonita's quick thinking saved Deanna's life and career, not to mention her sanity. Her kind personality was noticeable by a lot of the child stars in Hollywood. As the late Cora Sue Collins said, "She was the woman that every boy wanted to date, and every woman wanted to be."

Bonita's caring personality, and like the Aquarius she was, it wasn't surprising that she was

Bonita would help Durbin out another time, when Deanna called Bonita, crying. She was having marital troubles. Bonita, not yet married, but in a relationship with actor Jackie Cooper at the time, tried to put herself in those shoes.

"Bonita felt everything—if you cried to her, she was so empathetic," Gloria Jean said.

Deanna said, "The only reason why you want me here is so you don't have to feel guilty about my death in two years' time." Bonita's response to this would affect Durbin for the rest of her life: "Not guilt, I wouldn't say, but really sad. The hole you'd leave would be more devastating than the guilt that is ever left!"

In the time that Bonita said those words, Durbin slowly calmed down. Bonita's words hit her like a ton of bricks, because she knew that Bonita was right.

Bonita's gift for empathy seemed to come to her naturally. Though she was kind and empathetic, she was not naïve. Bonita understood the nature of her peers. Not everyone was kind to Bonita and she knew that, but did it bother her? Sometimes.

In a heated moment, when Deanna Durbin was going through her marital problems the first time, she threw this at Bonita, who was just trying to be a good friend, "Not even your own father loved you!" Helen Parrish and Gloria Jean, who happened to be there when the heated moment happened, were shocked at Deanna for saying such a thing. Bonita's father had passed when she was thirteen, and to Bonita, she didn't let it bother her too much, but the way that Deanna said it, made Bonita really stop in her tracks. Gloria Jean recalled the heated moment well:

> "Bunny stood there, in shock, but didn't yell back. She stood there, and took Deanna's words and her only reply was, 'If that's how you feel about it' and walked out the room. She cried herself to sleep that night. Deanna never formally apologized to Bunny about what she had said, but she did in other ways, but sometimes, Bunny took on the world and it was cruel to her. This is not to say that Deanna was a cruel person, she wasn't, she was just going through a lot and she didn't know how to handle it, so she took it out on Bonita. Durbin could be really mean, but Bonita knew that whatever Durbin said, she didn't mean, not in a malicious way," Gloria Jean said. Helen Parrish was shocked, but Bonita never held it against Deanna, in fact, she knew that she was just handling a lot, especially in front of the press.

Bonita also felt uneasy around her then-boyfriend Jackie Cooper's friends, and she knew how to judge a person by their character and a lot of these characters she didn't particularly enjoy. She knew who was fake and who wasn't.

"That was the best part about her! She could just sniff the fakeness and not want to be around that! It's like she was a bloodhound for fakeness! She wasn't particularly fond of mean girls, who just wanted to be cruel to others or want to steal each other's boyfriends," Ann Rutherford said in an interview about Bonita.

But sometimes, people thought Bonita was square— meaning dumb or boring. Bonita, in fact, was the opposite, she was full of life, but some people didn't realize that yet.

Bonita was in her own way, "wild." She loved going on adventures, she loved to travel and see the world. She always enjoyed seeing different cultures and trying new food, though sometimes she would be unsure of what some of the food was. She loved being with people, and that's what Gloria Jean recounted the most in her interviews and her phone conversations.

"She was incredibly social and she was the life of every party! She was that cheerful and that giddy. I loved being around her. Her energy was contagious and my goodness, she was a light in this world, and I wished that she were still around," Gloria Jean had said in an email in 2016.

Bonita really did love people and put her heart on her sleeve. She was sensitive, but she was kind hearted and loved by the ones who really knew her best.

Bonita with Jackie Cooper in Gallant Sons (1942): (Harry Ransom Center, UT)

"She was my whole world"—Jackie Cooper

CHAPTER SIX: JACKIE

YOU CANNOT TELL the story of Bonita Granville without the name Jackie Cooper popping up. Why? It's because they were once engaged and in love. Bonita Granville was 14 when she first met Jackie Cooper, then 15.

Jackie Cooper was born on September 15, 1922, in Los Angeles. He was the son of a vaudevillian pianist and songwriter. Jackie's career began in 1929, after his grandmother took him to the film studios and got him some extra roles. When Hal Roach discovered Jackie and put him in the Our Gang shorts, Jackie rose to prominence. He signed with MGM when he was 8 years old, and his first big film was *The Champ*, co-starring Wallace Berry. Berry had a reputation in Hollywood. He hated working with children and every child star that had worked with him, said that he was a god-awful man to work with. Jackie was no different. Jackie's success at MGM was very quick and he continued to star in string of hits, such as *Skippy, The Devil is a Sissy, Treasure Island, Tough Guy, Boy of the Streets and That Certain Age."* Jackie Cooper's roles from the time he was signed at MGM, were merely "family films," until he began to get older and he did "boyfriend roles," meaning he was always in love with the leading ladies. Some of his leading ladies, were some of his friends: Deanna Durbin, Susanna Foster, Peggy Moran (Koster), Judy Garland, Lana Turner, Helen Parrish, and Jane Withers. His uncle, was film director, Norman Taurog. Norman had directed successful films like, *Mad About Music (1938), The Toast of New Orleans (1950), and Skippy (1931),* which starred Jackie. Jackie Cooper was wild and free. At MGM, he was considered one of the most successful male child stars of the 1930s's. His career boomed from the time he was 8 until he reached 13. When it came to Bonita, his whole world changed.

In 1938, Jackie was introduced to Bonita for the first time, but it wouldn't be the last.

In his book, *Please Don't Shoot My Dog*, he described Bonita and their first meeting. "At the time I made *White Banners*, I was fifteen years old. I played a brainy kid, the illegitimate son of a housekeeper (Fay Bainter) in the home of a scientist (Claude Rains). Bonita Granville played Rains' daughter, and my character and Bonita's became very chummy. We didn't [date]. Not then. She was a year younger than I was, and after all, I was almost a man, I thought. I had watched Mickey Rooney palling around with twenty-year-olds and I watched Judy Garland dating thirty-year-olds, and I'd been friendly with Lana Turner and Ann Rutherford. At the time, too, I was very involved with Pat Stewart, who was a year older than I was, so I didn't give fourteen-year-old Bonita Granville more than a friendly hello."

At first Jackie thought that she was beneath him, a pest, and yet, she was the most vibrant person on that lot. Bonita had energy that not even Jackie could match. Her energetic and optimistic attitude seemed to attract his attention. Bonita's eagerness to please and work hard on the set, seemed to rub off on the 15-year-old Jackie.

Bonita's memories of Jackie were sometimes glamorous and then we have the memories that aren't. When Bonita was asked out by Jackie Cooper, in a way she was living her dream: Have a boyfriend, get married and have a family. That's all she wanted. As she said in a letter to Gloria Jean in 1946, "Jackie was perfect, and I wished we could have understood each other better!" Also in that letter, Bonita expressed to Gloria Jean that life wasn't always easy with Jackie. She wrote:

> "My dear friend, in time, I hope you understand that love can be such a fickle thing. I know with Jackie and I, when we were together, we had such good times, and yet, we had our fall. I believe that in every relationship, comes a give and take, and yet, love is so funny! It can come and go. You might think you love this guy, and yet, the way that he treated me, was almost a ying and yang. I got the

> good with the bad. Gloria Jean, my dear, I wish you find a man who won't be so difficult to deal with and I hope you don't have to do it in the public eye. Yours, Bunny."

Bonita's fascination with Jackie really began in 1938, when they made their first film together, *White Banners*. Bonita, being a good Catholic woman, was always taught that a young lady shouldn't sleep around. Bonita, being curious about her body, wanted to give Jackie all the love she had, within reason and within her limits. Jackie's book *Please Don't Shoot My Dog* describes his sexual escapades. The only woman he couldn't really conquer was her. As he mentions in the book, her mother spoke with him and said, "You're not sleeping with her." Bonita was torn. She knew that her other friends, like Helen Parrish and Judy Garland, were experiencing sex and here she was, a virgin with no real sexual experience. This frustrated her, as she wrote to Helen Parrish in 1943, "I want to experience what you have! I wish I could throw away this cross, but I know that is not what God would want!" Bonita's heart again, was split in two, torn between her desires and her public image. Her religious beliefs also contributed to her not wanting to just "hop into bed" with her first love. In a letter in 1947 to her dear friend, Gloria Jean, she wrote:

"I am glad that I waited, but I really was tempted by the virtue of sex, and lust. But I think at that time, what was I wrong to think those things?" In Gloria's reply, she stated:

> "No, you weren't wrong, you were in love with Jackie, what better man to start off your love journey." Jackie's book, *Please Don't Shoot My Dog*, is his autobiography that was written in 1981. He wrote about his life, and that included a lot of the love story of Bonita and him. The book itself is a hot mess. It seemed like he was complaining a whole lot, more than just telling his story. He does mention Bonita in there, quite bit.

At the time when Bonita met Jackie, she was caught between a girl and a woman. She was enamored with Jackie, and why wouldn't she be? Jackie was hot and believed it. She was thinking that she could really have a life with him. Jackie, unlike Bonita, lived in the fast lane. She was not keen on drinking or smoking, or both. As Jackie said, "Even then, she never drank or smoked." Linda, Bonita's daughter, said the same thing. Bonita unfortunately was around second hand smoke her entire life, and yet, she never had any desire to smoke. Jackie, smoked and drank, like it was nothing. He also experimented with drugs, something that Bonita never touched, even if she wanted to, she had no desire to.

"When Jackie and I dated, I'm sure plenty of the kids drank and did things they weren't supposed to do, but there was no dope, there was none around, you never really heard of dope and you really looked askance on anybody who got loaded regularly, falling down drunk; that was not the thing to do. We had fun-I basically would call it good clean fun, which young people in motion pictures, and out of motion pictures, don't seem to have much of anymore because it has to involve PCP or angel dust or something which makes people go crazy and you're a square if you don't smoke marijuana. Alcohol seems tame now compared to all these other things."

A lot of Bonita's parts in his books, are contradictory to what Jackie says. The reason this being, is because Bonita wasn't around for any of that. She didn't do drugs, and she didn't drink. She treated her body like a temple and she intended to keep it that way.

Jackie was the first boy that Bonita ever really loved, and it showed. In the 1940s they were America's sweethearts—they were mentioned in almost every Hollywood magazine. From *Photoplay* to *Motion Picture Magazine*, they were an item! In *Hollywood Magazine (1941),* the two love birds were the talk of the town:

> **"JACKIE'S GOTA GIR-RUL!**
>
> Jackie Cooper, fresh from a swim with Bonita Granville and some kids, was lying flat on his stomach near the pool, lazily scanning a Hollywood column while he let the sun bake him dry.
>
> Suddenly, his eye caught a paragraph in the column and he sprang up as though someone had given him a hotfoot.

"Hey, Bun — Bun," he yelled. "Did you see this? Don't pay any attention to it. There's nothing to it!"

Bonita read the article while she massaged her head dry with a Turkish towel. It stated:

> "Now that Jackie Cooper appears as Judy Garland's beau in Ziegfeld Girl, Bonita Granville had better watch out. Jackie is reported to want to duplicate this role in real life too."

"Oh, that," said Bonita calmly, still rubbing her damp head. "I saw that this morning. Pouf — doesn't bother me a bit." And in a lightning change of the subject she soon had Jackie telling her about the new maroon car he had set his heart on buying.

Which shows that these kids are not only the youngest pair of hand -holders in Hollywood, but also the sanest. Other Hollywood couples let gossipers tear the vitals out of their friendship. Jackie and Bonita have fun and trust each other. They won't manufacture trouble or triangles.

Based on such honesty and fair play, the friendship — and some call it love — between Jackie and Bonita shows more genuine dignity and balance than the more blatant Hollywood romancers who are older in years and experience.

Jackie and Bun, as he calls her, don't like to have their relationship referred to as a "romance," although if it isn't that, then Gary Cooper is a midget! They think the term is so final, puts it in a category with so many off-again on-again Hollywood affairs.

"It's so mushy," says Jackie gruffly.

"Can't we have fun together," adds Bonita wisely, "without people asking questions?"

In that way, Hollywood youngsters going through the thrilling experience of "first love" are on the spot. Try and recall your first crush. Just imagine the embarrassment and joshing you would have been in for if that first love-affair had been splashed on billboards. Being Hollywood notables, Jackie and Bonita must endure the billboard screaming's every time they go dancing, take a drive in the ribbon roads of the Hollywood hills or hold hands at a movie. They don't have much privacy, but they are making normalcy of that very cockeyed institution known as Hollywood first love.

Jackie and Bonita have known each other since they were young children. Both child actors, they were thrown together at various children's parties. At first, eleven-year-old Jackie looked down on ten-year-old Bonita who was "that kid" who wore ruffles. Bonita has always been dainty. Jackie is a rugged fellow who even today can't get into the habit of picking up his clothes. They didn't hit it off at first.

Later, Jackie and Bonita worked together in White Banners. Jackie's estimation of Bonita rose when he saw her do a particularly difficult scene. He told his mother, visiting the set, "She's marvelous. She's a young Helen Hayes."

As they grew older and began to move gayly in the small clique of Hollywood's younger set, Jackie and Bonita were thrown together at barbecue parties and jam sessions. Jackie and Bonita started to date each other soon after an outdoor party to which they were both invited. It was chilly for California, but a few of the hardier kids got into bathing suits and took a dip in the pool. Jackie was one of them. Bonita was another. He discovered that Bonita was a good swimmer and a swell sport in the water. Didn't mind a bit if her hair got wet or if she got mussed up.

These days you don't see Jackie without Bonita. Jackie doesn't like to be alone. If Bun is at the beauty parlor, he will pick her up there and take her with him to the saddle-maker's, to the tailor's or on any errand he's bound for.

But romance? The grande passion? Wedding bells? "Lay off," they both say, blushing. Let the kids have their fun.

Fun they do have, and that's why they continue to go with each other. But they don't make plans any more serious than where to go next Saturday night.

Jackie has always had a girl.

"When he was six," said his mother, Mrs. Bigelow, "Jackie was afraid Mitzi Green wouldn't marry him. Then he forgot her for Helen Parrish when he was eight."

They're seldom alone. Jackie and Bun are the ringleaders of the teen age clique. When they make a date to go to the Grove, usually they end up with a gang the staggering size of a Rotary group.

No matter where they go, Bonita phones her mother almost every hour. If it seems that Jackie is going to keep her out later than their twelve o'clock limit, Jackie calls up and pleads for more time. "Oh, c'mon, Mrs. Granville. Let Bun stay out an hour later, huh? I'll take good care of her, don't you worry."

There's an open camaraderie between Jackie, Bonita and their mothers. Mrs. Bigelow and Mrs. Granville have a lot in common. They have both raised child stars from tadpoles, and they have been through the same mill together. They have both had a tough struggle when the children were infants, and now, through their children, they are recapturing the fun they missed.

When Mrs. Granville had a birthday a month ago, Jackie slipped away from the table.. When he returned a few minutes later, you could see that he had accomplished what he set out to do.

When the cake was brought in, it was loaded down with 98 candles. Everybody screamed. Jackie looked at Mrs. Granville. "Why, Mrs. Granville," he told her, "you don't look a day over 97!"

An accepted sort of possessiveness passes between Jackie and Bonita that tells more than anything else, of their deep affection for each other. When that protectiveness shows a slight tinge of bossiness, Bonita loves it. She knows that only when a boy really cares would he take the sort of attitude that Jackie did right after he and Bonita came from the preview of their co-starring picture, Gallant Sons.

On the drive home, Jackie shook his head like a schoolteacher.

"Bun," he said, "There were a couple of times in the picture where you didn't stand straight. Did you notice?"

"A little, Jackie."

"Well, I don't know what I'm going to do about making you stand straight. You've just got to, Bun."

"Yes, Jackie."

"Look, tomorrow morning why don't you get a broom and hold it back of your shoulder blades for about a half hour. That'll do it. Will you?"

"You bet, Jackie."

Bonita likes to dress to Jackie's taste. Before Jackie, she used to wear fussy little clothes. Feminine dresses with bows and knick-knacks.

"I don't like clothes with thingamabobs on them," Jackie once said.

Suddenly, Bonita's clothes are minus the extra fuss. They're crisp and tailored; well-fitting suits with open neck shirts; angora sweaters and slacks of trim skirts. She doesn't wear her hair piled with a million curls on top of her head, but lets it hang soft in a shoulder-length bob. That's the way Jackie likes it.

On the other hand, Jackie likes to take Bonita shopping with him.

"How do you like this tie, Bun?"

"I think it's too icky. Now this blue one is so much smarter."

Jackie bows to Bonita's un-icky tastes.

Jackie takes a fierce pride in Bonita; thinks she's going to be a great actress when she's a little older. Being a man of many talents himself — he swings a noisy drum, can sing and do a time step — he was asked to contribute an act to a Chariot's Revue being put on for the benefit of the British War Relief. Jackie accepted, and then worked out a number in which Bonita could appear with him.

"But Jackie, I've never been on the stage before," she wailed. "I can't sing or dance."

"About time you did then. It'll do you good."

"But what will I do?"

"Don't worry. I'll show you." Jackie spent long hours teaching her the dance routine, happily threw the good lines to her, angled himself so that Bonita would get better lighting and position. They were the hit of the show.

"Bonita is adorable . . . never knew she could do that sort of thing." Jackie, getting the gist of the audience's whispers backstage grinned and pressed Bonita's hand enthusiastically. "See, I told you!" They both love swing music and go dancing Saturday nights. On that night they dress. They know how to do things up right. Jackie loves to smack away at the drums and most of the orchestra leaders know that. Invariably, they invite him to play a number with them, but they know that Jackie won't accept unless they send one of their own boys to dance with Bonita. Jackie won't let her be unescorted even for a moment.

That sort of boyfriend is one worth holding. A few weeks ago, when they both had a week off between pictures, they went to Palm Springs with their mothers. Jackie is a great horseman, Bonita is a little afraid of dobbins. The first morning there, Jackie asked Bonita to go riding with him in the desert.

Bun didn't want to admit that she was a little shaky about getting on a horse, so she told him she was too tired. "I don't think I'll ride while I'm here. In fact, I didn't even take my riding clothes," she admitted in a white fib.

A little later, she saw Jackie sashay off with three other friends, two girls and one boy.

As the foursome rode away, Bonita cupped her chin in her hand and did some thinking.

Bonita reacted as women through the centuries have reacted. Early the next morning, when Jackie called to take her to breakfast, he was surprised to see Bonita dressed in jodhpurs. "Funny, I found them in my trunk after all. You know," she said as they started off toward the stables, "I adore a ride before breakfast. Don't you?"

But came a situation just the other day about which Bonita could do nothing except to retire gracefully.

Bonita is working in Wild Man of Borneo and she plays the 18-year-old daughter of a Gay Nineties vaudeville mother who dresses Bonita as an 11-yearold to permit her to ride half fare. Bonita wears braids, an old-fashioned cotton dress which scraggles unevenly around the knees, and little makeup. Judy Garland, working on the same lot in Ziegfeld Girl is decked out in Adrian glamour didos and looks like a gorgeous doll come to life.

One noon-time, Jackie offered to take both girls to lunch. When he showed up to call for the girls, Bonita was nowhere to be found.

She couldn't bear the idea of walking into the commissary in her dated outfit with her best boy friend, while Judy was resplendent in the combined efforts of Ziegfeld and Adrian!

Which proves that comes love, teenagers know the ropes too!"

Young Love! The truth was that Jackie wanted more than Bonita could give him. He wanted to enjoy her in ways that she was not accustomed to. The way that Bonita felt with Jackie, as she put it, was "magnetic." She loved being with him. But there was one flaw: Was Jackie really all that enamored with her? As Bonita said about dating him:

"Jackie was really my first romance. Mother had always been kind of strict, and I never had a chance to date and go out and do things like that like everybody

else; they all started a little earlier than I did. So this [dating Jackie] was when I was about seventeen. I think Jackie had a couple of serious romances [before me]. I look fondly back on it because it was very glamorous."

In *Please Don't Shoot My Dog*, Jackie seems very bitter about Bonita and yet, you wonder why he dedicated an *entire* chapter to her. He very much needed to, as she was a big part of his life and for years, he held onto his bitterness about her. You would think, if someone was so bitter about someone, why would you write about them in your memoir, while they are still living?

When Jackie wrote in his book about how Bonita wouldn't do this or do that, she already knew what his intentions were. Bonita's own intentions—she wanted to be married and have a family and one day walk away from her career. She didn't seem to understand Jackie's fast lane lifestyle. Jackie was not always faithful to her either. He always seemed to have another girl waiting, just in case Bonita and him didn't work out. He was frustrated at her.

"Her mother was on all our dates," He complained. Bonita's mother was strict on her daughter dating and Bonita even recalled that.

Jackie was really my first romance. Mother had always been kind of strict, and I never had a chance to date and go out and do things like that like everybody else; they all started a little earlier than I did. So, this [dating Jackie] was when I was about seventeen. I think Jackie had a couple of serious romances [before me]. I look fondly back on it because it was very glamorous." Bonita never spoke ill of Jackie and yet, he bitched about her.

He continued his foul complaining:

Bonita's holy heart understood that she needed to be careful with Jackie. Jackie's drinking turned into violence. Luckily, Bonita was never struck, and if she was about to, she ducked.

She didn't know that Jackie was going through a lot of problems on his own. When his mother died, he was only 19, Bonita was there to pick up the pieces. As Jackie put it, she was comforting. Bonita's eyes for Jackie would remain for a long time, but for Jackie, it seemed as if he had other girls on his mind. Bonita's idea of love and marriage would be considered by some as traditional. The only problem was, Jackie was anything but traditional. He wanted sex, but Bonita was not at the time ready for any of that. She didn't want that "quick pace" as Helen Parrish put it in 1951. Bonita, to some, may have seemed square—in modern terms, boring—but Bonita became adventurous as she grew up. Bonita was not one to rock the boat, but at the same time, when she became more uncomfortable with the fact that Jackie would kiss her and sometimes slip his hands in her dress, she would quickly move it, and say, "My goodness, Jackie! Not now! Not until we're married!"

Funny enough, Jackie's plans for Bonita *was* marriage. But in time, it seemed as if he kept trying to jump the gun. Bonita's view of Jackie was more than just a boyfriend. At the time, Jackie was paired with Bonita yet another time, other than *White Banners*.

Bonita and Jackie were paired again for a teen murder mystery called *Gallant Sons* (1940), and their love seemed to blossom even more. Jackie was excited to be working with his favorite girl. In *Gallant Sons,* Bonita plays Kate, a school girl who, with the help of her friends, tries to solve a murder. Jackie plays Byron "By" Newbold, a teenage boy whose father works for a newspaperr that printed a story that affected Gene Reynolds' character's father. The two boys decide to work together to solve the case.

In the trailer for the film, Bonita was referred to as the "Girl in the Mortal Storm." Bonita's role was big enough for her to get noticed, but, at the same time, it seemed like the boys got more attention.

People seemed to understand that Bonita really didn't want the pressure of being a "star dust" girl. What she wanted was to be a serious actress, and for everyone to understand that she was changing, as well as her insides were changing.

She confided in Gloria Jean and Helen Parrish, that Jackie seemed to be a little fast for her, but, according to Gloria, things couldn't have been more different for the two of them. The ideals and morals of Bonita seemed a little too much for Cooper, though he stated that he did his best to love her. Bonita was full of love, and she had a lot of love to give, but she was not going to wait on any man in the armed forces, though during the war, she "dated" many servicemen.

Bonita's affection for Jackie was very apparent, but it seems that in *Please Don't Shoot My Dog* he writes about her in a way that doesn't seem so appealing. He makes her sound pathetic and overall boring. But the truth was, she was far from boring, she just had something that Jackie didn't have: a sense of morals. Bonita was so incredibly faithful to Jackie, and yet, he wasn't to her.

Gloria Jean, a friend and fellow actress who knew both Jackie and Bonita, said,

> "The problem with Jackie is that he was a boy, and most boys, on the lot, only wanted the girls for the stories, not even for their love. Jackie, I know, loved her, but was so incredibly frustrated, because she wasn't Lana Turner, or any other blonde that seemed to bring the boy's joy. Yet Bonita was different, because Bonita's heart was literally gold, and she was not full of herself. She didn't go to sleep with men, though she was photographed with a bunch of them. Just because she was photographed with them, didn't mean she always liked them. With Jackie, she did

everything she could to keep him happy and alive. When he started drinking, their relationship got harder."

In *Please Don't Shoot My Dog*, Jackie talks about Bonita in a way that seems so degrading, so you're thinking, didn't he love her? He did, but at the same time, his book was very bitter. Jackie had a very different view of Hollywood than Bonita did. Bonita's relationship with Jackie was exclusively public. They were the hot commodity that young people in the 1940s read about. Their love affair was even more complicated. Jackie had a little more experience in the business, even more than Bonita, but she dropped out first. She didn't seem to reach the same amount of popularity as he did, but she achieved more than he did in so many ways. The first was that Bonita had a great head on her shoulders. Jackie, technically, didn't have a father, and his mother died; Bonita didn't have a father either, but she had a darling mother, who raised her daughter to be the best woman she could be. Jackie, in many ways, envied his girlfriend, to the point of throwing her under the bus in 1981. Bonita was very much alive when the book was published. She never stated her views or commented on the book.

In 1939, Bonita and Jackie were engaged, but here's the kicker: Jackie wanted to wait until he was 21, which would have been in 1943. Bonita would have turned 20 in 1943. Bonita's love for Jackie was real, but she also saw a side of him that she didn't need to see. In a lot of old Hollywood stories, sometimes you hear about how men were drunk and terrible and yet, they were on the screen acting as if nothing was wrong. Jackie, being a young man, wanted to experience everything and, sometimes, that meant things that Bonita didn't really want to associate herself with, like drugs and alcohol. Bonita's squeaky-clean image would always be important to her, but not as important to Jackie. As he states, "Bonita was a saint, and yet, she put up with a lot from me." Bonita's affections for Jackie were exclusive, but she couldn't always wait for him.

When Jackie was drafted in 1942, Bonita's views changed. The way that he began treating her, sometimes, she thought, "Okay, I'm over it."

Bonita's letters to him still exist, and they are nothing more than a plea for him to "get your shit together"—said nicely. She said in a 1941 letter to him: "I don't know how much more I shall take of this. I need you to try to look at yourself in the mirror and see who the real problem is, cause I'll tell you, it is not me!"

As Jackie said in *Hollywood Magazine*: "But now there is the war, and that changes everything. In a few months—September, to be exact—I will be 20 years old, an age that makes me eligible for active service. I'm in good health and have no dependents. I expect to be called and to go. Like so many other fellows, I don't know where I'll be sent and when I'll come back. Let me say here that if, when I'm 21, conditions are normal and I'm still around, and if Bonita and I feel the same about each other, we will get married. But if I am sent away, then our marriage will be postponed for the duration. Bonita and I have talked it over, and there are many reasons for our decision."

In *Photoplay Magazine* in 1942, the question of their "marriage" plans were even disscuessed in a whole article:

> **"No runaway marriage for these two!**
>
> BONITA GRANVILLE and Jackie Cooper both love pointless stories and thick red steaks. They both have quick tempers and a genius for saying the wrong thing at the wrong time. And they both believe, heart and soul, in old-fashioned weddings with all the romantic trimmings.
>
> "No runaway marriage for me," said Bun.
>
> "Elope? Not me," said Jackie.
>
> Both were quick to point out it was their personal opinion they were expressing, not an indictment of recent Hollywood newlyweds who had chosen to dash off on sudden impulse to some distant town and surround the marriage ceremony with semisecrecy. If others like Judy Garland and Dave Rose, Gene Tierney and Oleg Cassini, Kathryn Grayson and John Shelton preferred eloping, then elopements certainly were right for them. It simply was a matter of how Bun and Jackie, as individuals, felt on the subject.

Immediately, too, they insisted they were speaking about marriage in general, not when, how, or even if they themselves get married. Not only have they never 'announced any marriage plans, Bun and Jackie said, but actually they never have made any such plans. Cross their hearts!

"It's silly to talk about marriage when we're not even old enough to vote," Jackie explained. "Seems to me it would be a smart idea if we finished this growing-up business first. After all, I've just turned nineteen and Bun's even younger. We've got lots of time ahead of us." "Check!" Bun amended. "And there's another reason — our careers. Each of us happens to be at a pretty important point in our professional lives. If we are to win the success we want, our first interest and consideration must be for those careers, not marriage. I don't believe you can get married and then say: 'Well, that's that; marriage will take care of itself so now I'll devote myself to my career.' Successful marriage doesn't work that way, particularly for a girl. It has to come first and neither of us is ready as yet to pigeonhole our screen work in a place of secondary importance."

Jackie grinned. "Lady," he said, "you said a smart mouthful!"

They do admit to being boy and girl sweethearts and have been for well over a year. Bun thinks Jackie is tops, even if he does squander his allowance in an atrocious fashion, and Jackie rates Bun as aces, even if she is disgracefully careless about being late for appointments. And maybe, when the time is right.... BUN first met Jackie when she was a giggly fourteen, during the making of "White Banners." She got her first nod from him on her fifteenth birthday — a bottle of perfume for a birthday gift. It was expensive perfume, too, in keeping with Jackie's belief about doing things right if you do it at all. Then, apparently, he forgot anyone named Bonita Granville was on earth.

Eleven months later, she saw him again. This time it was at a "jam session" at his house, and two of his best friends, Buddy Pepper and Junior Coghlan, were her escorts. The evening was memorable to Bun for one reason: Since she had nothing in the musical line to contribute to the "jam session," Jackie ignored her completely in favor of his beloved drum!

The day before Christmas (almost a twelve-month lapse this time!) Jackie telephoned around seven-thirty in the evening and asked for a date that night. Bun began to demur in the expected feminine' way; it was "awfully late" to be asking for a date.

"You're not doing anything, are you?" Jackie demanded point-blank.

"No," Bun admitted. "But — "

"Then let's go," he said. They went. Dancing at the Beverly-Wilshire to heavenly music and complete forgetfulness of anything like a clock. Bun got a scolding for being late but decided it was worth it. Christmas day Jackie appeared in company with her other swains, Pepper and Coghlan, and gifted her with a charm bracelet made of flags of all the nations.

It was some time in March he again telephoned and asked if she would like to go with him while he made a layout of publicity pictures of bowling, swimming, ice skating and so on in the afternoon. Bun accepted and promptly amazed Jackie by honestly enjoying the various sports and proving herself remarkably proficient at them. Here, he decided, was something pretty swell in a girl.

"Do you have to go home now?" he asked. Bun said no.

"Then let's have dinner and go to the preview," he suggested.

After the preview he again asked if she had to go home. She said no.

"Then let's go to Ciro's for a while." As he left her at her door, one thought was pounding in the back of young Mr. Cooper's head. He had been in Miss Granville's company for a solid twelve hours and darned if he wasn't wishing there were twice that time still to go.

THEY started dating once every, two ' weeks. Then it was once a week. Then it was twice a week. By June of last year (1940) they had reached the daily telephone-call stage and were "going steady." Since then neither has dated anyone else. Not that they ever had one of those "we will" or "we won't" agreements. Both believe such decisions label one as youthfully naive. Rather, they just slid into a tacit understanding.

Daytime dates, when picture schedules will allow them, are given over to swimming, horseback riding and bowling. That's one reason they're both so excited about working together in "Syncopation" at RKO; each will have free time at the same time. It was tough going when Bun was making "H. M. Pulham, Esq." at Metro and Jackie was crosstown doing "Glamour Boy" for Paramount.

Evenings they have dinner and go to the movies (both are movie hounds) or stay home and play phonograph records. On Saturday nights, as a rule, Bun and Jackie step out in style. The best times, however, are those dates when they sit and daydream about former dates.

"Heaven help me if I get a July night mixed up with a September afternoon!" Jackie said. "Bun has a memory like an elephant. Doggone, if she can't remember everything I said six months ago and why I said it!"

"Heaven help me if I keep him waiting ten minutes for anything!" Bun laughed back. "Jackie is a positive maniac about being on time!"

They have made all sorts of interesting."

In the1942 edition of *Hollywood Magazine,* the issue of marriage also came up and this was said in the article:

"MARRIAGE MUST WAIT!- JACKIE COOPER

"Shall we marry now?"

Throughout the length and breadth of the land, thousands of young men who are off to war and the girls they will leave behind are asking that question.

In Hollywood, a strapping, wavy-haired young man and a blond slip of a girl sat down one evening and gravely talked it over. The boy was Jackie Cooper, the girl was Bonita Granville. "Jackie and Bun," the most publicized of Hollywood's younger romancers. Of all the love affairs blooming in cinema town, the wholesome, unspectacular courtship of Jackie and Bonita is the one more representative of the rest of America than it is of Hollywood. Here, then, is how this American couple are approaching the problem facing so many other young men and women today.

"We decided," said Jackie simply, "that marriage must wait."

Jackie was doing the talking for the two, slightly red-faced and uncomfortable, feeling that this was Bonita's province. Nevertheless, he spoke frankly, revealing a hard-headed masculine viewpoint.

"Bonita and I," he said, "had planned to be married next year, when I would be 21. We have known for some time that we were in love and wanted to marry, but in spite of the prodding's of the gossip columnists we weren't hurrying it because we were both too young. We always said we wouldn't marry until I was 21, because it would be rather silly for me to try to be the man of the house when I wasn't even considered a man in the eyes of the law. However, we used to talk about it now and then, even agreeing on the kind of wedding it would be — a church ceremony — and the sort of ranch home we'd live in and arguing about whose dogs we'd keep. That's how it stood.

"But now there is the war, and that changes everything. In a few months — September, to be exact — I will be 20 years old, an age that makes me eligible for active service. I'm in good health and have no dependents. I expect to be called and to go. Like so many other fellows, I don't know where I'll be sent and when I'll come back. Let me say here that if, when I'm 21, conditions are normal and I'm still around, and if Bonita and I feel the same about each other, we will get married.

"But if I am sent away, then our marriage will be postponed for the duration. Bonita and I have talked it over, and there are many reasons for our decision. Neither Bonita nor I think it's feasible to start out in marriage with an absentee husband. Now I know that this theory doesn't hold water with a lot of people, but those are our views. It's trying enough for a girl who has been married a few years to say goodbye to her husband, but at least those two have had some time together. But if we were to get married on the eve of my going into Uncle Sam's service, we would be courting trouble.

"I don't think it would be fair to Bonita. She would be stuck in Hollywood with no one but her mother as a companion, for Bonita has very few girlfriends. Hollywood, being the town that it is, would clack its tongue if she went somewhere escorted by another man. In other cities, girls may be squired by an absentee husband's friend with no reputations ruined, but try it in Hollywood and inferences are drawn! Why, just look at this," said Jackie, fumbling in his pockets and producing a frayed two-line news item, which said that some other boy had replaced Jackie in little Miss Granville's affection. You see, he laughed, I was away on a personal appearance tour and Bonita had dinner with a mutual friend — and, I might add, at my suggestion. Immediately, the trouble-makers started mooching in. Bonita and I shrugged it off, but it wouldn't be so easy if I were in the service and such rumors were to start, for a wife faces greater criticism.

"I wouldn't want Bonita trapped like that. If I have to go away, I would like her to be able to have a little fun. That doesn't sound as though I'm very jealous, does it?" he grinned. "I am, however. If I thought another fellow was crowding me. out, I'd burn. But when you've been going with a girl as long as I have been with Bonita, and if you know that she's fine and true, you're not going to worry about her chasing around with other boys the minute the old back is turned.

"I don't mean to be smug. Anything can happen, and there's always the possibility of another fellow appearing on the horizon and winning out over me. But if such a thing should come about, it would be better for all concerned that there be no ties to break. Then no one gets hurt. Bonita and I have never seriously gone with anyone else, and some people have told us that we should go with others to prove our own feelings. We don't need such a test, and we're not anxious to have one. I have had only too many occasions to know what a wonderful girl Bun is. But if a 'war separation' is forced upon us, then when we get together again and find that our feelings are the same, marriage will be all the more right for us.

"Besides," said Jackie thoughtfully, "there's this danger: war changes a fellow. The experiences he undergoes, the emotional and physical upheaval that takes place in his system when he is transplanted from a peace-time community into actual warfare, does drastic things to him. I see friends of mine today who have been in the service for a year and their entire philosophy is changed. They're more restless, their ambitions have been reversed. I hear that in the last war when the soldiers came home, they couldn't stand to live at home anymore and had little in common with their old friends and interests. That might happen to me, too. Right now, I feel that I want to stick to pictures the rest of my life, doing character roles on the Spencer Tracy type as I grow older.

Bonita agrees with me. But suppose the war knocks those ideas out of me and changes my whole personality? And suppose Bonita doesn't see eye-to-eye with the changed person I have become? We think it would be unrealistic thinking to get married when such an emotional transition faces us.

"Bonita and I have thought it over and we've made our own decision. Maybe some people will think we're overcautious. Judging by the great number of war weddings, there are a vast number who disagree with us. On the other hand, Mrs. Roosevelt, who has a deep understanding of the problems of young people, warns against hasty war marriages. It doesn't matter to us which view is the more popular, we think we're doing what is the right thing for us. We would be presumptuous to try to recommend our way of thinking to others.

"Now that we've arrived at our decision, we don't talk about it anymore. There's no sense messing up a nice evening by glooming about the day when we'll be separated. We want to enjoy every moment of the time we have together now. At the moment, we're both busy in war work. We're doing all we can for War Bond sales and Army shows. But I can't wait for the day to come when I am asked to do more — when I can do a man's job for my country in bringing this war to a victorious finish.

"Then when it's over, I hope Bonita and I can pick up where we left off. But," he said slowly, "not until then."

That being said, Bonita already had her sights on another man, or should it be said, a few other men. One of those men was actor Tim Holt. Bonita was not one to just sit around and wait for her Prince Charming—she wanted more out of life. She wanted to be loved and be touched.

According to Gloria Jean, who knew Bonita well at this time, she said, "Jackie and Bonita were like the Justin and Selena of their day. But sometimes, Bonita wanted more. But Jackie was wild! He wouldn't slow down!"

In the time that Bonita was trying to figure out if Jackie was really what she wanted, she soon realized that she could marry Jackie when he returned from war, and they could be happy, but as she said, "Some things could have worked out, but knowing where Jackie was headed, I could have been dead."

Jackie's mother died in 1941. Even with Bonita being by his side, his personality began to shift, and according to Gloria Jean, "Jackie's treatment of Bonita became hostile. He turned to the drink and sometimes she didn't know how that would impact her, but she certainly understood that she couldn't take much more of it."

Bonita understood that Jackie began drinking, but she didn't want to let him know that she knew. In one letter she sent to Helen Parrish in 1943, she wrote, 'He told me to get out! To get out before he killed me!"

Bonita had told Gloria Jean the same thing, and to that, Gloria replied, "She had never been so scared her entire life." She tried to be positive, but even at that time, Gloria Jean recalled, "Bunny did everything she could to make Jackie happy, but I could see how their relationship was crumbling quickly."

Bonita realized that he was on his way to war, but she wasn't going to be the stay and wait kind of girl. When she was making *Hitler's Children*, Tim Holt seemed to be the replacement Jackie for the time being. Tim Holt was a few years older and, to Bonita, he seemed to have a good head on his shoulders. Jackie, unlike Tim, seemed so much more interested in Bonita. Bonita's letter to Gloria Jean, in 1943, reveals how much she wanted more out of Tim: "He's much more intellectually intelligent and to be blunt, I wouldn't mind slipping off my dress for him."

Bonita's sights on Tim were more than anything that she could have managed. In her exclusive interview, "My Wartime Morals," published in *Photoplay* in 1943, she said, "Neither of us would admit this at first. Our love had been so sweet and we couldn't bring ourselves to relinquish it. For years we always could be sure of the same quick response from each other. But when we came to our late teens, it was different. Personality traits that had us bound together, began receding. Personality traits which found us basically at variance for the first time in our lives began strengthening. Quite literally as Jackie and I grew up we also grew away from each other."

Sometimes, when you read these articles, usually the stars are speaking in code. This means that they mean one thing, without really giving the full details. So, when Bonita said, "Personality traits which had bound us together began receding. Personality traits which found us basically at variance for the first time in our lives began strengthening. Quite literally as Jackie and I grew up we also grew away from each other"—here's the actual translation of that: Jackie's personality has begun to shift and he's turning to alcohol, and he's going to hurt me. He was drunk, but the problem was, he was underage. Drinking really turned Bonita off and nobody really knew why.

But, the problem with Jackie, being off to war, is that Bonita realized that she could be in serious trouble if she stayed with him while he was drinking, and she was right. Before he went off to war, the last thing he told her was to get out before he killed her. He had been drinking, and according to Gloria Jean, he was drunk and he threw something that was glass at her, but luckily for Bonita, she had amazing reflexes and ducked before it hit her. She knew right then and there, that their relationship was *done*. That was Done with a capital D. She wasn't about to be a victim like some of her counterparts. She was over him, and yet, she wanted nothing but the best for him.

Knowing Bonita, she knew when somebody was kidding around and serious. In this instance, Jackie was serious. She knew that her days with Jackie were numbered and, in that case, she sought to find something else, and with that replacement came Tim Holt.

About Tim, she stated in *Photoplay*, *"It was after Jackie and I faced the fact that it was over for us that I thought for a time I loved Tim Holt."* She continued, "It wasn't, however, until we worked together in *Hitler's Children* that we really knew each other. Tim had separated from his wife. He was sad over this, feeling lost, too, because his marriage meant a great deal to him. He was eager and emotional over this. I, no longer wrapped up in my love for Jackie or his love for me, was

unhappy and lonely. Not only were Tim and I sorry for ourselves; we also were sorry for each other. I'll never smile again—as you do at an old bromide—when I hear anyone say, 'Sympathy is akin to love.' I found out! I know now this has been sold over and over because over and over it has been true. Tim and I came close to making a serious mistake." Translation: *"Tim and I nearly had an affair."*

Luckily, for Bonita, Jackie was well on his way out of her life by 1943. When he returned to the United States after the war, Bonita's attitude towards him really shifted completely. As Jackie said in his book, *"Bonita didn't like musicians. She kept talking to me, very seriously almost as a mother would, about the 'company' I was keeping."* He then went on to say, "Especially after my mother died, she began to adopt a very maternal attitude towards me." She cared about Jackie a great deal and didn't want to see him go down the tubes, but as she said later, "He did that on his own, he didn't need my help."

With the films they made together, *White Banners*, *Syncopation* and *Gallant Sons*, their love bloomed. It seemed after *Syncopation* (1942), things started getting more haywire. Bonita saw a different side of Jackie that many people didn't. The thing about Jackie is that he was smart, but at the same time, he thought Bonita was too motherly. Bonita only wanted what was best for him, because, apparently, nobody was looking out for him. Though Jackie's words about Bonita in his book weren't always kind, she still showed up for him. In 1994, Jackie Cooper did an interview for TCM (Turner Classic Movies), and he didn't mention Bonita once! The interviewer didn't even ask him about her, which is ironic, because they dated and were once engaged. So it was little odd, that she wasn't even mentioned. Jackie died on May 3, 2011, at the age of 88 years old. He outlived Bonita by 23 years…

Jackie Cooper with Bonita -1941(Author's Collection)

Jackie Cooper and Bonita out on a date (Author's Collection)

Bonita Granville with other child stars at Judy Garland's party, 1939(Author's Collection)

Bonita's publicity portrait in 1940 (Author's Collection)

Bonita on a date

"She was Bonita Granville, the woman was a saint, but my GOD, she could be petty when needed to be! "— Freddie Bartholomew (1924–1992)

Chapter Seven: "Boy Bye!"

It's amazing when people think that everyone in old Hollywood liked each other. Newsflash, they didn't. Bonita was no different. There were a few people that she didn't care for. She didn't particularly enjoy Lana Turner, though she was always polite and kind. People tried to pit her and Judy Garland against each other, but that never really worked, since Judy and Bonita adored each other. In the late '60s, Bonita quietly paid some of Judy's bills [1].

"One thing that Bunny hated was when people acted holier than thou," Gloria Jean said. Bonita's reputation was always trying to keep her squeaky-clean image. She was kind, gracious and, sometimes, that put people off, which never made any sense. Bonita was also a very faithful Catholic and usually could tell who was not good to hang around with. Luckily for Bonita, she had a good head on her shoulders and being a good Catholic woman who had morals and values, she wasn't a woman who slept around, and as she said herself in an interview in 1974, "I wasn't a woman on that couch." She was referring to the casting couch, a term that means that women usually slept with producers, directors or even actors, to get parts in films, and that could include getting movie contracts to rival studios. Bonita was not that kind of a girl and sadly, there were actors who thought she was. She might have been beautiful, but she had respect for herself and for her own good, she managed to evade scandal.

One way she did this was to always be around people she knew wouldn't cause a fuss. Ann Rutherford, who was a contract player

1 According to Gloria Jean

at MGM, understood Bonita's plight and point of view. When Bonita was signed at MGM in the 1940s, the two became fast friends and were photographed constantly for publicity portraits. Ann always described Bonita as a woman who really knew who she was. "She had thick skin, but I think the most important thing about Bonita was that she had an enormous heart and wanted to have fun, the right way." Ann was like Bonita in a few ways, they were always both overlooked and seemingly queens of B pictures.

The thing was that the men of the 1940s were usually treated with more respect than their female counterparts. The women of the era were sexualized because it was what sold and Bonita, sadly, was in that position. During WWII, Bonita was considered a pin-up girl and yes, there are plenty of pin-up photos of Bonita (they're easy to find!). Bonita was always trying to keep an open mind when being a teenager or a young woman. She wanted to be seen as a woman of good faith. A woman who did good things, who helped her mother and did charity work. To Bonita, the war effort seemed to be the priority and she

In some films that Bonita made, especially when she transitioned to MGM, she became the woman who men lusted after. One man in particular, who Bonita knew very well, would try to say that she needed to sleep with him, or he could ruin her. This man was Mickey Rooney (1920-2014). Now, say what you want about him, he was a man who thought he ruled the MGM lot, because he had been at MGM for a long time, he was box office gold and he was, according to child star Freddie Bartholomew, "a raw talent." But under that surface was a man who thought he could get any woman to sleep with him.

Ha! So he thought! Bonita wasn't going to play that game! She knew it, but sadly, he didn't. When they were at MGM together, Bonita remained generous and she knew that if she didn't play her cards right, she would not be utilized. MGM was notorious for signing these wonderful women, and then putting them in roles that they were not suited for.

Bonita first met Mickey when she worked with him in *Ah, Wilderness!* (1935). "I knew Mickey then, and he was energetic then, but as he got older, he became fuller of himself and that wasn't very fun to be around," Bonita said.

Being a great actress, Bonita understood that she had to hide her feelings from the camera, but if you watch her body language in the film *Andy Hardy's Blonde Trouble*, you can see how kind of put off she is by him. She was approached by him in ways that she was not comfortable with. He said he could ruin her if she didn't sleep with him. As Helen Parrish recalled to Gloria Jean[2,]

"Bonita was approached by Rooney, and he said that if she didn't fuck him, he could ruin her. She laughed and said to him that she could ruin him before he even touched her!" Bonita was not one to give in to peer pressure. She felt that she could think on her own and she didn't have to have a man to tell her who to sleep with. She didn't need that then and certainly didn't need it later. Bonita's worth was more than some of her contemporizes. She didn't care if she was box office gold like cohorts, such as Shirley Temple or Elizabeth Taylor. All Bonita really needed was to get her energy out.

But Bonita Granville was a part of the Studio System in old Hollywood. That usually meant that they picked the roles for you and if you didn't take them, you were put on suspension. Suspension was something you didn't want, believe it. She took the job and she thought that Mickey was going to be his same old self, happy and goofy. What she got was the opposite of that. She tried to make it perfectly clear that she was not interested in his advances. She told him as kindly as she could that she was running out of nice ways to say go jump off a bridge!

She went out to lunch with Ann Rutherford that afternoon, asking her friend what to do. "Don't worry, Bunny, I've had to work with that man over 10 times. Every time an Andy Hardy film is made, I usually have to work with him, so don't stress about it." She didn't.

When Bonita went out to lunch with Helen Parrish and Gloria Jean that next day, still pondering on what to do when Rooney approached her again, Helen Parrish said, "Don't worry, beautiful, he's just an asshole!" Bonita then said, in a rare fashion, "I'm Bonita Fucking Granville!! Who does he think he's talking to?!"

2 Gloria Jean recalled this in a phone conversation in 2015

As Gloria Jean recalled, "Helen and I just sat there, with our drinks in our hands, looking at her with such surprise and shock, because everyone knew that Bunny Granville never cussed or swore! If she did, you must have pissed her off!" Bonita simply looked at her two friends and said, "Revel in it, ladies, it'll never happen again!"

In the time span that it took Mickey to realize that Bonita was a lady and not like the other women he'd known, she was not easy for him to get in bed. She had better morals than that. Though it was odd, she was usually surrounded by men who thought she could easily slip under the covers. Nope, not Bonita. She would go on dates with men, but they weren't actually dates, just publicity stunts.

As Gloria Jean said, "We were set up on dates for the world to see that we were 'in love,' but in reality, many of these men weren't worth Bunny's time!"

Bonita Granville was the most eligible woman in all of Hollywood between 1943-46, according to all the old Hollywood magazines.

The men who wanted her basically wanted her for two things: The Name: Sometimes when people married in old Hollywood (it still happens today, sadly), they marry said person for the "name." Let's give you an example: When Deanna Durbin married Felix Jackson, or Vaughn Paul, they married her so they could be "Mr. Deanna Durbin." With Bonita, she knew this, and she was not interested in someone being "Mr. Bonita Granville," at least not at that moment.

The Money: Bonita Granville made money, and by today's standards, she'd be more than a millionaire, but men wanted half of that.

But at the time, men in Hollywood felt they could do almost anything to women and get away with it. Bonita was a little different than her counterparts. Helen Parrish said in 1952, "It's amazing how Bunny survived and she made something of herself!"

In the space and time, it took Bonita to shake hands with a man who wanted to take her out for the night, usually to be photographed, or be spoken about in the tabloids, she was actually trying to keep her sense of clean imagery, while being a good woman of faith.

Bonita Granville with Gloria Jean during a radio program

"It's okay, Kate, even Bunny Granville, one of the happiest and sweetest women in Hollywood, cried too"—Gloria Jean.

Chapter Eight: "It's Okay, Bunny Cried Too"

"Hollywood can be a real lonely place," Bonita once wrote. It really could be. Hollywood was a place where people came to make their money and then go home. Bonita really was a social person. She loved being the life of the party. As Freddie Bartholomew, a child star in the 1930s and early '40s said, "Bonita Granville sparkled and believe me, she loved the spotlight! She loved being in it! She was so warm and so friendly!" But Bonita was what people didn't think she was: Human.

In 2015, Gloria Jean recalled a story about how human "Bunny" Granville was: "It was 1943, right after Bunny and Jackie parted ways. I don't think people understand that the people in those pictures were *real.* We had *feelings.* We had *emotions.* We were going through things that the public knew nothing about. Bunny Granville sometimes was lonely. Everyone gets lonely. I have a story to tell you, and I know this doesn't sound like her, but it's one of those things that the public never knew.

> When she and Jackie parted, it was really hard on her. Any break up is hard, but especially when your breakup is in the middle of the public eye, it's even harder. She was so upset that she cried herself to sleep some nights and even when she was taking a hot bath, as she told me. She was a loving woman, but even underneath that "tough exterior" was a girl who wanted to be loved and adored. It's harder than it looks. It was hard to imagine a woman like Bunny Granville, who was so lively and so warm, to ever have been sad. I knew her when she was sad. She was

a woman who had real feelings, and she understood what to publicize and what not to publicize. With this, she didn't feel like she was getting enough love or support. I certainly was going to give her some. She called everyone that she knew of, and I guess they weren't answering or weren't able to be with her, but she finally rang me up and said, "Can you come over and have cake with me? I know it's last minute!" I stopped her right there and said I was on my way. I arrived at her house, and, Kate, I kid you not, her eyes had looked so red from crying. I immediately hugged her and at that time, we were relatively the same height. She invited me in. She told me that the cake was vanilla, she hoped that was okay. I told her, as long as I got to spend time with her, anything worked! Trust me, Kate, you would have wanted to spend time with this gal! The sweetest little woman, who took pride in her love for others, just like somebody else I know. It's okay, Kate, even Bunny Granville, one of the happiest and sweetest women in Hollywood, cried too, and sometimes, she had every reason to do so. She was sometimes overlooked, chewed up and spat out. That's what Hollywood did to these kids, chewed them up and spat them out.

Now, we ate in her dining room and she cut the cake for us. I don't know why she got it, maybe to make her feel better? Or maybe she got it to try to not make think so much, I mean, Bunny loved food, but she didn't over eat. She ate modestly her whole life. She took care of herself her whole life, at least that's what I recall at the time. When we sat down to eat, she started talking about how she was happy that I was there. We talked about everything, and you wouldn't believe it, but she was *human* (I know! What a concept!). She had emotions, she had feelings, and she really wanted to be loved, just like every person on this Earth. It's amazing Kate, how she was this petite woman, that had so much spunk to her and yet, when the world turned it back on her, she didn't turn her back on it. But with Jackie, there was major heart break here. He was the first boy that she ever loved and the first boy that she really ever dated. Her mother, at the time that I can recall, was a thin woman, who really was kinda strict. She didn't really let Bunny do a whole lot of things that we other kids got to do and I know she felt a bit ostracized by that. I know she told me that she was really allowed to date, and felt a bit oppressed by that, but she didn't really complain about it, she said that she envied us all, which I could understand. She told me that after she and Jackie parted, she felt utterly alone, and though you wouldn't have guessed that, it because she was always being photographed with other men, but she felt so alone, and to be blunt, Bunny Granville was the friendliest and the most positive woman, and it was so hard to see her like that. How could this charming woman, who was then a young woman, feel so alone, and yet, while being photographed with other men, look so happy? That's called publicity, but I knew, as she told me, when she came home, she would cry her eyes out. She told me that Jackie was her first love, and how could your first do this? I recall how warm she was. She was beautiful on the inside as well on the outside. She didn't know what to do. She said, "I don't know why Jackie was like that! He was so .. I am really not sure what to do about his career, Gloria, he'll ruin that himself!" Little did we know, he did, for a time, but Bunny understood how he didn't mean to ruin himself, he just had a lot going on. In those days, kiddie actors were merely the breadwinners for their families, and Bunny was no different. Bunny's kindness was usually thrown back into her face, and believe me, she took on a lot of shit from sooo many of those kiddie stars, who thought they were all that and a bag of chips. They weren't, not a single one of them! Some of those kiddie actors ended up broke, destitute, or ... dead. Not Bunny. She ended up rich, kind, successfull and, not to mention, not on drugs! She never went off the rails and she was always so gracious. Sometimes, people like Lana or Hedy would try to overshadow her, but Bunny was a shining light all her own. Anyways, we were sitting there at the table, eating that vanilla cake and her voice was sweet, but she was shaky, Kate. She didn't know if I was going to judge her for her decision on breaking the engagement with Jackie. He was not the best at that time. He was going through a lot and I believe she tried to keep her spirits up, because that's the type of person she was. She was always positive, and if she cried, she had every right and reason to do so. I always learned so much from the people that I knew in Hollywood and one thing I learned from her is that being a good friend goes both ways. Listening and reciprocating is something that she always did. Like you, she showed up for people, even if they didn't deserve it. I know this for a fact! If Judy [Garland] needed something, best believe, Bunny would show up. Sometimes, just being there for someone can make a *huge* difference. Bunny and I sadly lost touch over the years, but I knew Bunny. When I called her before she passed, she sounded much different. She didn't sound like herself, but she was sick, and I didn't know the extent of how sick she was. She had just lost Jack [Wrather] a few years before, and she was on her own. But, in reality, she knew she wouldn't be too far behind. But she told me that she "had a cold" and she'd be okay. She died later, and, Kate, when she died, I cried for hours. That woman, who did so much for everyone, was now no more. The world lost its light that day, and I believe, the world hasn't been the same without her. I still think of her every now and again, and I smile every time. That woman was everything, and she really was a great asset to Hollywood. She really was a wonderful person, and I cannot say enough good things about her. I know you and I have a special bond with her, and I'm sure she's guiding you to be just as sweet and wonderful as she was!

I really recall that day when we had cake and we got to really talk. I knew so much more about her heart, and believe me, Kate, she was, and still to this day, one of my

> favorite people that I ever got the chance and honor to know!"

Sometimes, the audience watching these films tend to forget that the stars on the screen were *real* people. We tend to forget that they had lives. They dealt with illness, and sometimes they dealt with mental illnesses as well. The kiddie stars of this era were going through their own growing pains, only except they were doing it on the screen and in the public's eyes. Like Bonita Granville growing up in front of the screen, most kiddie actors felt that they were the realization of their parents' unfilled dreams. Bonita sometimes felt that she was her mother's unfulfilled dream, and yet, she never complained and she went along with everything.

As Gloria Jean recalled in another email, about how Bonita Granville felt "insecure" about herself. Bonita wrote to Gloria Jean a letter in 1943. She wrote:

> "Gloria, it's hard being famous. Sometimes, I don't even know if it's worth it. Sometimes, I feel like when I look in the mirror, I'm looking at a fake, a phony, but it's just... me. I know she's me, but there are times where I feel like I don't like the girl standing in the mirror. She's pretty, but she's also in front of the cameras most of the time, if not all of the time. The way that I feel, is that I cannot express my emotions in the ways that I would like. I want to tell people who I am, and the way that I was raised, was probably a little different than most, but I promise Gloria, I.. I have a difficult time realizing that I'm there? Is it me? Am I really Bonita Granville that the world all knows and loves? Of course! That's me, right? I would hope it is. I can't express the problems that I have to anyone, since they would say, Bunny you have it all! Why you must badger and complain? I am nothing more than a commodity, a thing that seems to make these senseless men money. That's all I feel like sometimes, a cash cow. But what of you? I know you and Deanna {Durbin} have that voice, and yet, do you not get tired of it? Do you not feel like someone could one drop you like a hot potato?

> I had this horrific dream last night. I dreamt that I was out of work and on my own. I know how to do that, but I... didn't have a home and no one would ever hire me again! Oh Gloria! How can my mind come up with such talk? Or such things for that matter? How? I am blessed beyond belief and wealth, and yet sometimes, I am envious of the women who seem to be the top favorites, and yet, here I am, trying to understand everything about this business that I've been in since I was a kiddo! There is a lot of sadness and tragedy to it. Is there not? Am I just babbling or am I right? God, I don't ever question, but yet, I have many questions about why I am not being answered? Am I crazy? Am I? What is going on with my mind? Is the devil trying to tempt me? I am trying my best get the best answer from the Bible, but I haven't found any comfort. I am scrambling around trying to get my answers. But my God, I feel like I am going mad! Anyways my dear friend, there is much to be grateful for! Best, Bunny."

Gloria Jean had kept all of Bunny's letters. They had exchanged quite a few after they first met in the early 1940's. Bunny's charismatic smile and personality impacted the then 14-year-old Gloria Jean.

"She was the kindest woman and believe me, I've met a lot of fakes in Hollywood," Gloria Jean recalled on a telephone call.

Gloria Jean was kind enough to type out one of Bonita's longest letters she sent in 1944. Gloria typed in the email, before she had pasted the typed-up letter in the email, she explained that that Bonita was going through a "crisis," but not a midlife one, just an internal one.

A "crisis" that all actresses go through, a crisis of oneself, confidence and what the future holds. Gloria told me that this letter, seemed unlike her, because in her view, "Bunny" was usually calm and collected and never, ever worried about anything. But what Gloria didn't realize at the time, was that Bonita was going through a lot of changes of her own, and that meant, sometimes she worried, but as she usually did, she reached out to those friends, like Gloria Jean, who would be there to listen to her and comfort her.

In this letter, Gloria Jean had stated that it was really the first time she saw a "raw" and "vulnerable" side of Bonita. Gloria Jean said that it was really the first time that Bonita Granville, showed her that she was really a person, and not just the woman on the movie screen that we all knew and loved.

"May. 2, 1944.

Dearest Gloria,

I have so much to say! First thing's first, how are you? How is everything? I have so much to explain! First off, I think that we need to get together soon! Second, I hope your sisters are all well. How is your mother and father? I hope they are also well! My dear friend, I know I can come to you in confidence, as I have already spoken to Ann {Rutherford}, but I also wanted to come to you. Gloria, my dear Gloria, I feel stuck. Yes, me Bonita Gloria Granville, is worried and stuck. I haven't felt this way since I was 12, and now, I am here again. I'm frightened about my future, especially in pictures. Where would we go when they {The Studios} don't want us anymore? What will become of us then? Do we become the homeless women on the streets, or do we become the regular homebodies that once had illustrious careers? Dear Gloria, the fears that I have, that I keep inside of me, are now growing and I am trying to stop them before they get out of control!

I think of those fellow actors and actresses that came before us, where are they now? Are they has beens? Is that we will become? I already feel like that already, and I'm not even 30! I guess what I'm saying is that, I wish that God could tell us what our future holds, even if it means that I won't be an actress anymore. Are you afraid that your voice will give out? I am scared for the world, especially because we are in a war, not just with the world, but I feel like ourselves. What price tag does fame really come with? I have been trying to understand the world we live in now. I pray that God will have a way to stop this war, or stop the cruelty of the world. Gloria, I have been blessed beyond belief, and yet, there is something I'm trying to find? I have everything. I have a house, a loving mother and lovely career, and yet, I feel a little empty. I read my Bible, and I go to Church, and yet, I'm finding myself, lost? But what is there to be ungrateful about? I have everything I could ever want, and I know I have many people to share my affections with, but in this moment, I feel undeniably, lost. I don't know if it's because I feel like I'm just a "character" actress, or I'm just trying to figure out where my talents will truly take me? Gloria, you have that voice, that gift, I hope you do not squander it, for you are a talented singer, but I hope you understand the predicament that I'm in? Sometimes, I feel like I'm living an out of body experience. Have I done all these things? I don't know? But yes, that is me, Bonita Granville, in the mirror and in front of the cameras. I've been in front of them since I was 8, and I'm now a woman. The changes that one woman goes through in her lifetime astound me. It really is a challenging thing for me to go through. The world expects so much of you, and then, what is left for you? What do you expect of yourself? I have so many questions, that I feel like only God could answer. (turn page over). The biggest question that I have, is what did God intend for me to do? I know sometimes I have these thoughts, of existence and what became before me or what will become after me? Is there such a thing as losing faith? I believe in Jesus and in God, but do I really understand what God has in store for me? I don't know why this is bothering me so much, but I feel (turn the page) like I'm starting to feel like I'm slipping away from things that are really important to me, such as God. We trade our morals for the next best thing, whether that'd be our morals or our beliefs. I'm not sure why that's always bothering me, but is. I don't feel like I'm existing in the once world of make believe, that I know I've always existed in and yet, it's making question my abilities to still even work, or perform. How long must I go on like this?

I mean, I enjoy the profession, but at the same time, the roles aren't coming to me, nor are they really roles I want. I know Mr. Mayer says that there are no small parts, only small actors, well, I'm small anyhow, and yet, I have the smallest parts! I don't want to act in another role with Rooney, and I don't want to be the ...girlfriend. I know my Nancy Drew days are over, but I can honestly say, that I am growing up, and one day, I will be playing roles that are meant for me, or one day, run them! I don't know Gloria, sometimes, I feel so lost in this world, and yet, I'm barely a woman. The roles that we women are given, are now. Sometimes I feel, are not great. They're just. Boring Maybe that sounds too selfish of me to say, or ungrateful, but honestly, don't they have any roles where women are empowered? Or do the men feel that they want us to be the "little girl" or "girlfriend" forever? Gloria, you and I are growing (turn the page) up and there's a lot of worlds we need to explore. For one thing, we are growing up as young women, and what does mean for us in this industry? I know once we reach a certain age, that we're done for, and what does that teach young women who want to go into this profession? Make sure you're young and cute, and you're not willing to grow up. I'm sorry Gloria, I'm just frustrated at everything. The way that people treat us, the way that women are treated. The way that just because we're aging, we're discarded... as what? As cardboard? As? What? Those are the thoughts I have on my mind Gloria, the thought that one day, I will too, be nothing in this world, then just ... a has been? Mary Pickford went through and I know Shirley {Temple} is too. What is to become of us? Are we just glitter until we run of that? What are we Gloria? I'm trying not to cry on this letter, because I have legitimate fears .

What will become of us, in the time and space that we are able to showcase our talents? What happens when they're gone and no longer useful? What if no one will hire us again? We have to make our own way, I know it,

> but really, what is happening to us? What is happening to me? Am I lost in this dream that I cannot wake up from, or what is that keeps me going? Yes, God, and Jesus, and the faith that I hope will we someday be able to reach that place where there is God. I don't know what you believe, but I always have believed in the hope that God will make the world a better place. As for the industry, I hope things will change, but I pray that it will. Women, I feel like have stronger voices than most. We have been through so much Gloria, and I can understand why it is so difficult for men to understand why we just want to be like everyone else. Women are powerful. I wish that people would see how strong we are together.
>
> As I sit and write this to you, I wonder if my anxieties are alleviated, and somewhat they are. I hope that you do not find me to be a bother with all this. Well, I know I'll be getting something to eat, and I will mail this to you. Best, Bunny."

Gloria Jean had always said that letter in particular was one that she would read often and the reason behind that, is because, Gloria had the same fears. *What would become of them after they were discarded by Hollywood?*

Another time that Gloria Jean and Bunny met, this time for dinner was in 1945. Bunny had just completed a B film, called *The Beautiful Cheat,* a film that she told Gloria was juvenile, but it paid. Gloria at the time was also working on a B film, *Easy to Look At.* When they met, she noticed that Bunny was the same as ever, but she had *grown wiser.*

"I guess that's what happens when you've been in the business as long as she had," Gloria Jean recalled. Bunny had been in the business since she was 8 years old, and hadn't stopped working since.

"I think I might take a vacation," Bunny told Gloria Jean. She asked Bonita where she thought about where she wanted to go? Bonita said, that she wanted to go to the Galapagos Islands.

"I've never been Gloria and I wanna go! Oh! How I would love to go to the Caribbean too! Or the Hawaiian Islands!" Bonita had told Gloria. Little did Bonita know that Gloria Jean would eventually live in Hawaii.

"What else do you want to do with your future?" Gloria Jean asked. Bonita, as Gloria Jean recalled, said:

"I hope to marry a producer, and maybe create a charity!"

Gloria Jean laughed at that comment, and said, "What kind of charity?"

"One for the underprivileged children!"

Gloria Jean recalled that Bonita Granville was perhaps one of her favorite people that she had ever met in Hollywood.

In Bonita's final letter to Gloria Jean, in 1947, Bonita's tone was much more hopeful. Gloria Jean was also kind enough to type that up too:

> "May 1, 1947,
>
> Dearest Gloria Jean,
>
> How I have some news for you! I am in love! Yes! That Wrather man I was telling you about! I remembered what you had told me and I am so ever grateful! My thoughts of him being newly divorced had me concerned, but I know his children are extremely precious and I've taken to them nicely. Yes, dear Gloria Jean, he has children already! Two! A boy and a girl! I think they are just precious! I know that once I'd get to know him, I do think he'd be the perfect husband for me! I know he is a man who has a good head on his shoulders and he is from Texas. He is trying his hand at producing pictures, and luckily, I've been able to be part of them!
>
> You are right! Sometimes our hearts do talk, and when I reached out to you to ask your feelings about him, you helped me open my eyes! Thank God for you! Gloria Jean, I really cherish you and I hope you have known that! The heart and soul in which your body beats, is always loved and I am forever grateful for. My Gloria Jean, I will always be in debt to you. Sincerely, Bunny."

Gloria Jean always said that she regretted not keeping up with Bunny in their later years, but that letter that Gloria sent to Bonita for a reference for Television shows, Bonita jumped at opportunity to help her dear friend.

"She sent the best reference letter, and she remembered exactly who I was," Gloria said in an interview in 2016.

Gloria Jean said she always she remembered Bonita's kindness and warmth.

Bonita in full uniform with her puppy Chin Chin (Author's collection)

"People at the canteen, they got to see their favorite movie stars!"

Chapter Nine: The "War Woman"

During World War II, Hollywood went to war. Hollywood was doing everything they could for the war effort. She did her part at the famous Hollywood Canteen. The Hollywood Canteen was created by Bette Davis and John Garfield in the 1940s, the point of the canteen was for Hollywood to give back to the troops during the Second World War.

Between the years of 1942-1945, thousands of Marines, Army, Air Force and Navy men walked through the canteen, met by some of their favorite movie stars and singers. Deanna Durbin, Linda Darnell, Barbara Stanwyck, Gloria Jean, Anne Shirley and Ann Miller were among the stars who appeared at the Hollywood Canteen more than once.

On October 3, 1942, the Hollywood Canteen opened. Bonita jumped right into the war effort. She attended many nights at the Hollywood Canteen meeting with friends, such as Ann Rutherford, Linda Darnell, as well as Gloria Jean and Deanna Durbin, and dancing and enjoying her time with all walks of life at the canteen. Bonita's job at the canteen was quite simple: Dance with the servicemen, or give them food or just enjoy being the entertainment. Bonita's own image would don the walls of servicemen overseas. She was a "pinup girl," and Bonita wasn't always sure on how that would come across. As she wrote to Gloria Jean in 1943, "I'm not a gorgeous woman, but I guess if it's what these men want, then I shall do my part to help out!" Bonita's greatest joy was to go out on some "dates" with service men and make their day better. She understood the sacrifice it took for these men to go overseas and fight a battle to save the world. In time, Bonita

Granville was part of the war effort, and she did everything that she could to help.

In some of the footage that was filmed at the canteen, Bonita is spotted, dancing right behind Deanna Durbin. It may be for a brief moment, but she's there! Bonita Granville did more than just dance and entertain soldiers; she went on dates with them.

She even began a magazine column called "Your Problem and Mine," in which fans would send in their questions about anything to Bonita, and she would answer them. Bonita's column was very popular, in fact, Bonita answered different questions about all kinds of topics. Many of the submissions were sent in by young women, as young as 10 years-old. There was no age limit on the submissions, and Bonita got a ton of them! She thought it would be a great way to connect with her fans. She would be able to see what her fans needed help with, or what she could do for them?

An example of one of these columns:

> "Dear Miss Granville:
>
> I am a girl who will soon be eighteen and people say I am pretty, but I am shy and suffer from an inferiority complex. Especially with boys. I have had very few dates and each one was awful for me to go through. Somehow, I don't seem to be able to talk and can't find things to talk about.
>
> My education is average, and I know conventional subjects to talk about, but they never seem to fit into what the others are talking about. I want to have a good time, but somehow, I don't seem to fit, and I don't want to miss the "teen age" fun. It seems I will if something isn't done about me soon.
>
> Can you help me?
>
> Sincerely.
>
> Madeleine."
>
> Bonita's response to the submission, was this:
>
> "Dear Madeleine:

I well remember when I felt just like you do, and sometimes even now that same old feeling still happens to me.

I am eternally grateful for the advice given me by my mother on this subject. It has worked out beautifully and which I hope will help you too.

Mother carefully explained to me that an "inferiority complex" was the sign of a selfish and lazy person. She said that to meet people and to have them like you meant you must make a tremendous effort to please them. She told me how to be a good listener. This isn't easy, for you must be able to listen intelligently and to be able to ask the right questions. To be able to ask the right questions means you must be well informed on the subject under discussion.

I know a "date" is a very important thing to every girl. However, remember when you go on a date that you are going for mutual fun and your pleasant reaction to the happenings of the evening are your way of showing the young man you are happy in his company.

If you are natural in your reactions to things going on about you, you will have a good time and so will your companions. Try harder, be more natural, and if you don't know everything they are talking about, ask a few questions. Remember, everyone likes to be an authority. Work at being a friend and 1 am sure you will find your "inferiority com plex" and shyness will vanish.

Cordially,

Bonita."

Some of Bonita's column submissions dealt with issues that not many people would talk about, such as disabilities. In the 1945 issue of *Movieland* magazine, she replied to this very special submission.

"Dear Bonita:

I am a girl suffering from infantile paralysis. The disease left me with one leg shorter than the other and my left arm is not as mobile as it used to be. I am luckier than most people who get this dread disease, for I can take care of the leg problem with built-up shoes and no one notices my arm too much.

However, I do have a problem. It is one of pity. Everyone is especially careful around me not to call attention to my infirmities. It is very embarrassing for I would not notice them myself except that everyone is always making a special and noticeable effort not to notice them, which really does call attention to my trouble. Thus, I find myself not wanting to go out and meet new people.

My family do everything to try to make things easier for me at home, and I am perfectly capable of doing my share, but when I try, I suddenly find myself sitting down and being waited on. I don't want to hurt people's feelings for they are trying to be kind, but they are more of a hindrance than a help.

What would you suggest that I do.

Sincerely,

Marie P."

"Dear Marie:

Your attitude is to be admired and I am sure you can work out your problem yourself. If I can help you in this letter 1 shall be happy and hope you will let me hear from you again.

I would talk frankly to my family about their desire to help you and explain your wishes more thoroughly. Don't let them make a cripple of you. Your fine spirit proves that you are not.

Another thing I would suggest is that you find some charitable work. Perhaps you could answer the phone at a USO or Red Cross, anything that will get you out of the house and meeting people who will help you be more independent. I feel that your outside activity will give you the freedom from the hindering help of sympathetic people.

My kindest wishes to you.

Cordially,

Bonita."

Other topics that Bonita answered about was about *dating*. Here are a few examples of those submissions. Now keep in mind, this in the 1940's and people tended to get engaged, and get married, at a younger age than they do today, so some of these may come across as "far-fetched." But back then, this was the norm.

"Dear Miss Granville:

My boyfriend is in camp in the South, and I write to him every day.

He writes wonderful letters to me, saying he still loves me and all that, but the problem I have is that he also writes the same kind of letters to my sister.

Also, he always mentions her in the letters he writes to me, and it makes me furious.

Do you think that it is right for him to write love letters to my sister when he is engaged to me?

Sincerely

Ann."

When Bonita got this one, she knew in her heart of hearts, how to reply:

"Dear Anne:

Evidently the boy is not in love with either of you if he continues to write love letters to both of you simultaneously.

Why not try answering his letters with a lighter, more general style the next few times, making them less personal and newsier and chattier, the way you would write to an old friend — and then see if he answers in the same style.

If so, then you can be sure he is glad of the opportunity to slip out of a serious relationship with you, and you will be. spared the unhappiness of having this happen during your next meeting with him.

Sincerely,

B.G."

"Dear Bun:

I am sixteen and have a problem to ask you about. I have been going out a lot for the last six months, and people are beginning to talk about me.

You see I neck with the boys. Nothing bad really — just kissing. I don't see any harm in it. It really doesn't mean a thing and I can't see why people think it is so terrible. After all what is the harm of giving a boy a couple of kisses after you have had a nice evening with him? I think you should show him that you had a good time and then he will ask you to go out again. My girl friend thinks I am a fast stepper and I tell her she is wrong. What do you think?

Yours truly.

Geraldine."

Bonita's reply:

"Dear Geraldine:

I think there is no harm in kissing a fellow you like very much However, 1 do think it is right to be choosey whom you kiss. Remember, you may like another fellow tomorrow, and another the next day, and your life will become a kissing bee unless you watch out.

I always believe that a man places a woman on a pedestal. It is the woman who climbs down, not the man who drags her down. Men are meticulous creatures and like their women to be fine, pure and clean. It has been this way since the world began. Who are we to change it?

Goody-goody girls are dull, but a nice natural girl who is a good companion is what the boys really want. I am afraid if you go on kissing all the boys you will find that they kiss you and take the other girls 'out. Save your kisses for your nice future husband and learn meanwhile to be a companion to boys.

Sincerely,

Bonita."

This one was particularly telling of Bonita. She knew that being a "Good-goody girl," was almost "dull" for her time. But, in fact Bonita was a "goody-goody" girl, very rarely every broke any rules and never caused as rucks or fuss. But, Bonita would "break rules" every now and then.

Other topics that Bonita would speak upon were things like "Job interviews" or "Wanting to be more helpful!" Or even how to "Write better letters!" Here are some examples:

"FIRST INTERVIEW

Dear Miss Granville:

I am graduating from high school this year. I'm a commercial student, and I am going to look for a job. With the shortage of good office help I am sure I can get a salary of thirty dollars a week instead of starting at the usual eighteen-fifty.

One thing that worries me though, is how to apply for a job. I just don't seem to be able to bring myself to even apply. There are so many dos and don'ts in the instructions our teacher gave us that I am scared.

Another thing, I am not as pretty as most of the girls and I am sure that I will have a handicap in that. What do you do when you go to interview for a job in pictures?

Sincerely,

Caroline H."

Bonita's reply:

"Dear Caroline:

The foremost thing you must remember is that you are looking for a job, not going out on a social occasion. Your future employer is looking for efficient help in his firm, not for a pretty dinner companion.

You should dress simply and nicely, have your hair dressed in a becoming and plain manner, and conduct yourself quietly and efficiently.

State your experience or schooling simply, tell the truth about your ability and be objective in your statements. Rather than say, "I type well, but my shorthand is only 100" simply tell him your typing is excellent and your dictation is 100. Leave out the "only."

A trick I have, when I am nervous on a job interview is to take a deep breath as I enter the room. It seems to give me a confidence. I remember, too, that I am applying for the job, not the boss.

Lots of us are not as pretty as other girls but by taking advantage of our best features and having a reasonably pleasant nature, we get along. Everyone can't be a raving tearing beauty and lots of other things count much more, so stop worrying about your appearance.

Yours truly,

Bonita."

The "Stop worrying about your appearance" part of this submission, she felt very strongly about, due to the fact that her profession was literally based on "looks" alone.

"BETTER LETTERS

Dear Bonita:

This may seem strange to you* but I want to know how to write a good letter. Most of my friends are overseas and I try to write to them all the time but I don't get answers from them. My girlfriends get replies and I know it is because I don't know how to write a proper letter. I have read your answers in Movieland to the letters sent in to you and they seem to hit the point, so perhaps you could tell me what is wrong with my letter writing. Enclosed is a letter that I wrote to a boy overseas. What is wrong with it? I think my problem is one that many other girls have and maybe you can help us.

Thank you sincerely.

Mary R."

This one, Bonita really took into account:

"Dear Mary:

The trick on a good letter is to be interested in your subject. In a friendly letter you should write as you talk. If you talk well then, your letter will be interesting.

Don't write letters unless you really feel the urge. Write with a sense of humor and with your mind on the things that will interest the person who is going to receive it.

It seems to me when you write to boys overseas, you should tell them what has been happening at home. Write the things that are cheerful and forget the sad or unpleasant things that are going on. Try to be breezy and interesting.

Your enclosed letter was a good one, but a bit stilted. The next time you write make believe you are talking. You'll find that a big help.

Write often. The boys overseas need the letters.

Yours truly,

Bonita."

"She really should have been a therapist!" Actress Cora Sue Collins recalled about her friend, Bonita.

Bonita seemed to understand people very well and yes, she was a *therapist*, just not one that got paid professionally. She was therapist to many of her friends, who needed advice.

Here is another example, of Bonita being, just that..

"WANTS TO HELP

Dear Bonita:

My name is Ralph and I am ten years old. I wondered if you knew of anything that I and the boys in my gang could do this summer vacation to help the war effort. My mother says we can't go away on vacation this year but that we must stay home because of the war.

I thought you might know of something that little boys could do. We may be little in age but we are strong enough and big enough to do something that would help the war and keep us busy and maybe even earn some money.

Could you think of something we could do?

RALPH AND THE GANG."

Bonita's reply is just as elegant as she'd always been:

"Hello Ralph:

You sound like the boy who lives down the street from us. He had your problem and this is how he solved it. He has been collecting paper for the scrap drive. He helps with his school collecting and then does work with the neighborhood group.

He told me the other day that he was working hard on his arithmetic so he could work in the grocery store this summer helping in the vegetable stand. He is going to run errands and do lots of things this summer that the older boys have done before.

Talk to your mother. Perhaps she will have some suggestions, or perhaps your daddy may be able to tell you what you should do. Discuss this with them, and I am sure they will be able to tell you what you can do.

My love to you,

Bonita."

In the beginning when Bonita started these columns, she didn't write out her name, she just put her initials, B.G.

The first ones, are mainly about love, and the war, since when she started these, there was a war going on.

"Dear Miss Granville:

I have been engaged to a soldier for three years, and twice when he was home on leave, he begged me to marry him. I wanted to wait until I graduated, however.

Now this is my problem: he no longer writes to me — the last letter I received being in April — and an old friend of mine just came in town and he tells me that my fiancé is married to a girl near the camp where he is stationed.

I have cried and bitterly regretted that I didn't marry him when he asked me to. What do you think I should do?

Jean."

Bonita's reply was very interesting. She didn't understand why a boy that said that "he loved you," would just run away. However, she knew that she was with Jackie Cooper at the time, and he was drafted into the war, and she expected nothing less.

Dear Jean:

First, you were perfectly right in waiting until you finish school before thinking of marriage.

I can't believe that this boy sincerely loved you if he married another girl.

Perhaps you are really better off being rid of him, under the circumstances.

> Why not go out with other boys and enter into a new social life in your town? It may be hard for you now; but you have to forget him and that is the best way to start.
>
> Good luck.
>
> Sincerely,
>
> BG."

In a lot of these, Bonita does her best to try to reply with grace, kindness and above all, patience, just like a therapist. In a couple of the early columns, she addresses a lot about marriage and relationships, a department she knew something about. She wasn't married then, but she was in a relationship. She knew that relationships took work and they weren't always easy. Not everything was seen in "black and white."

> "Dear Bonita:
>
> I am engaged to a soldier, and he is nineteen and I am seventeen. But his folks think we are too young to get married. Also, we are of different religions, and my folks say we can never be happy being married with two different religions in the same house.
>
> What do you think we should do?
>
> Catherine."

One can only imagine the look on Bonita's face, when she read half of these, and had to respond in the best way she knew how. Particularly questions such as this, in the case of Catherine, being too young to marry, which in our view, yes, they would be too young, but standards were different then and Bonita, had to make a quick decision on how to answer this one:

> "Dear Catherine:
>
> You are very right in realizing these problems that face you, and in not marrying at such a young age.
>
> It is always happier to discuss such problems with both parties' parents, and try to reach an amicable decision. While people do marry without their parents' blessing, I

am sure it is a hap¬ pier situation to try and discuss the many phases of these troubles together with your parents and reach a happy compromise.

Sincerely,

BG."

Bonita's questions were from young people from all over the United States, hoping that their favorite actress, could help them out. In Bonita's view, she seemed very satisfied while helping young people out. Some of them, like the one below, she had to think about her response real hard.

"LOVE QUESTION

Dear Bonita:

Here is my problem, and it won't be an easy one for you to solve for me.

I am a young girl of eighteen and considered very pretty.

In high school I had had no special boyfriend, but about ten months ago, I met a very nice looking and fine boy, whom I grew to like very much.

We have had very few dates together, for he works, and I have to help my mother at home after school, but we do see each other at the baseball games and sometimes the dances at school.

I don't know whether to see him anymore, for he has grown very fond of me, and our religious faiths are not the same. He says he is in love with me, but I haven't told my mother, for I am afraid she will tell me not to see him anymore.

You are a young girl like myself; I don't know your faith, but surely you must have some idea what I should do.

I know I am young, and this may just be an infatuation, but I don't think so, and to lose him would break my heart. My mother knows him and likes him, but doesn't know how seriously I like him.

Flora."

When Bonita read this one, her heart shattered. She knew what it was like to be in love. She had Jackie at the time, and the thought of losing him, was Earth shattering, however, she swallowed her pride and replied:

Dear Flora:

First let me tell you that the reason we are fighting this war is that all people may be free and equal. We are fighting race and religious prejudice.

From your letter, I gather that you two have no intention of marrying right away, but you would like to plan on it.

I think you should whenever you have the full permission of your parents and his.

You should talk to the boy and explain your feelings about your religion and listen to his explanation about his. You both are deeply religious, I can see, and I am sure you will be able to work this out each with deep respect for the other's faith.

Your parents, naturally, should be consulted; explain to them how you feel, about your love for this boy, and that you realize your religious feelings could upset your marriage, unless it is all understood before. I am sure they will understand, and if they don't, talk to the pastor of your church and have him talk to them.

I sincerely hope I have helped you with your problem. Let me know.

Cordially,

Bonita."

This really stumped Bonita, but she makes several great points. The reason why America was fighting, was to fight evil and she knew that better than most.

One of the questions she got, she had to sit back and literally say, "Fuck you," in the nicest way possible.

"OVERSEAS VET

Dear Bonita:

I have just returned from overseas and have a very great problem.

I am twenty-one years old, and the girl I am engaged to is eighteen. We have been going steady with one another for a year before I went into the service.

Before I came home, her letters became fewer and fewer, and I couldn't understand, for she used to write to me about three times a week.

When I came home, she welcomed me as if I had never been away. She was still in love with me. Finally, I got her to admit the reason she hadn't been so prompt in her letters. It seems that, after I went away, she went out with a boy in the army stationed near our home. She swears nothing happened, but people in town talked. She finally didn't go out with him anymore, but people kept on talking about her. She swears they were just friends, but somehow, I doubt her, and I wonder if we should get married. I haven't told her how I feel about it, but I do think I should tell her I don't believe her. After all, marriage is based on mutual trust, don't you think?

Yours sincerely,

John A."

Bonita looked at this and decided to "kill him with kindness."

"Dear John A:

Yours is not a pretty problem, and it makes me a bit cross with you. It is hard for a woman to make a mistake and admit it, and your fiancée has done it. Are you going to depend on idle gossip to settle your life path or the girl you are in love with?

> Remember you, yourself, sometime in your life have done things that you regretted, but when you owned up to them, you found yourself a wiser person.
>
> It seems to me that your girl has been honest with you, and also that your doubt is hurting your relations with her.
>
> Why don't you sit down and talk to her? Tell her of your doubts and that now you know she was honest, and you regret your feelings that you felt you must tell her. Through this, you should have a new understanding, and your marriage will work out.
>
> My every good wish for your happiness. Congratulations in getting such a fine and honest girl.
>
> Sincerely,
>
> Bonita."

She felt relieved, knowing that one day, she too would be married, and marriage, as she knew from her mother's experience, was never perfect.

During the war, Bonita was photographed numerous times at the Hollywood Canteen, as well as doing bond tours across the United States with other stars. Part of the publicity circuit, from speaking at rallies or helping out with social security, the woman made her rounds to everything and everyone. Being a "war bonds girl," really took her stardom to a new level. Bonita did everything she could to help out the war effort and she always would be reminded of that much later.

Bonita, 1943 (Gift of Emily Evans)

Publicity for Hitler's Children *(Harry Ransom Center, UT)*

"Regardless of warning, the future isn't so scary at all"—Hikaru Utada

Chapter Ten: *Hitler's Children* and Life of the Party

In 1943, Bonita Granville took a role that really put her on the map, like Nancy Drew had years earlier. The director was Edward Dmytryk. In 1942, Hollywood began making anti-Nazi films. The film was called *Hitler's Children*, about a woman named Anna who sadly is caught between love and war. She is undoubtedly killed at the end, a shocking ending for that time.

Bonita Granville was always described as the Life of the Party. Her activities usually involved dances, parties and personal appearances; the latter arranged by the publicity departments of the studios.

The publicity department was quite amazing back in those days. As it was said, the more publicity you got, the more money you made. The more money you make, the more you got to eat, pay your bills, and live in your house. Bonita knew this, and she took plenty of opportunity to be the It Girl or play the publicity game, even if that meant being with men that were too old for her, or too grimy, as she called it, but she did it. Bonita never complained, and if she did, she usually would call up her old pal, Ann Rutherford, or occasionally she would chat up Helen Parrish, or Gloria Jean. These women had been through the ringer, just like she had, only difference was, when you were on a publicity tour, you were on your feet more than 12 hours a day.

Bonita did so much that the publicity department couldn't keep up! She was here! She was there! She was everywhere! The interesting thing was that Bonita seemed always ready to put on a show and get out there. The money that she made from all this publicity seemed to prepare her for the rest of her life, being in the spotlight. She understood her role, as an actress and as a public figure. What she didn't realize was preparing herself for public service for the rest of her life.

When she began the press tour for *Hitler's Children*, she was welcomed to all the major cities, where she was lavished with cakes and flowers. But in reality, she was doing her due diligence as an actress and to promote the film; in those days, you did a press tour, which is like the press junkets stars do now for their films. But back then, press tours meant you literally went across the country, on a tour to see crowds of people, to watch your new film. This sounds very exhausting, and overwhelming and best believe that Bonita felt all of this when she was promoting her film *Hitler's Children.*

Bonita was the star, and for once in her life, she was treated like one. The crowds came to see her, she was given many, many flowers (one in each city) and she had a busy, rigorous schedule.

She was exhausted and, yet, she had to perform. She had to keep her energy up, with very little sleep in between. Sounds difficult? You bet! It was extremely difficult to try to be in a lot of places at once, but she did. She drained herself of all the negative press or the negativity from other magazine hounds.

The problem with this was that this could have exhausted you and raise your blood pressure. Luckily for Bonita, she knew how to manage her time wisely. The first thing she did was try to see what was most important. For example, if there was a charity event and a special appearance that same day, she'd pick the charity first, then she'd rest for a few hours and then head to the special appearance. Bonita was an excellent planner. She knew how to manage her time and she knew how to manage it wisely. As Gloria Jean would always say, "That women was always working! She never took a break, or least it didn't seem like one! But she never ever bitched about any of it! I feel like she loved the publicity and most women back then, really didn't. But she was different, she took it with grace and poise. Her mother didn't teach her that, she did that on her own, that I'm sure of!"

Bonita's energy was sometimes described as an energizer bunny who wouldn't turn off. She loved the spotlight and she managed to stay in it for over thirty years. With each new press tour, she would gain the confidence that she would soon teach her counterparts, Deanna Durbin and Gloria Jean, to be in front of the camera. She loved being in front of the camera and it really showed. In every photograph that Bonita took, that big wide smile would appear on her face. That grin that she had, would dawn the covers of magazines and magazine articles. Bonita tried to understand that the world of publicity was like a game. She knew that if she didn't play their game, she would end up on the wayside. So, she did what every star did, she played the game, she ate the caviar, and she went on dates with men that she would rather not touch with a ten-foot pole. The woman was a pro, and in her later life, she became even more so. She strived for perfection and that's what she got. She never shied away from interviews or posing for a publicity portrait, whether that would be a studio shot or for her adoring fans, which, she had plenty of.

Bonita Granville was an absolute professional. In any case of a crowd, she seemed to keep her cool and try to breathe through her panic attacks. Bonita's anxiety would heighten if there was a large crowd surrounding her, and it wasn't because she hated crowds, she didn't, but she was worried for people's safety, not really for her own. Bonita would have some kind of body guards, to make sure she wouldn't be a target for assassination or kidnapping. Who would want to hurt Bonita? You'd be surprised, but luckily, nothing ever came of that kind of situation. Bonita's success with *Hitler's Children*, seemed to bounce her up to stardom. Bonita Granville was a star, it's just took this blockbuster hit to really make her one, and yet, she was a star all along.

In some other people's views, Bonita Granville didn't make it big as Katherine Hepburn or even Audrey Hepburn, and yet, Bonita is remembered for some of the biggest films in history, such as *Hitler's Children* and of course, being the first Nancy Drew.

Publicity for Hitler's Children *(Harry Ransom Center, UT)*

Bonita being the life of the party

Bonita taking a break on the press tour of Hitler's Children

Bonita getting a valentine (Harry Ransom Center, UT)

Bonita reading her contract for RKO (Author's collection)

Bonita in a Fashion Publicity for MGM (Harry Ransom Center, UT)

"As a child, everyone had a great investment in you not changing and then as you got older... you changed. And if this profession no longer worked for you, if you couldn't find a job, because you were growing a mustache, or you were developing as a young woman, and you obviously weren't what you had been, when you were a hot commodity, that could be very difficult. This investment that everyone had, in you not ever changing, and not knowing how to do anything else, is I think the thing that's been most responsible for all the folks with our backgrounds and our professions, who have gotten into trouble later"
—Dickie Moore (1925-2015)

Chapter Eleven: Not a Little Girl Anymore!

When Bonita became a teenager, she was trying to sell herself as a serious actress. She was one and, yet, people brushed her over, like she was a rug. Bonita's star status was not something to be reckless with. Her talent was *there*. When her time at MGM came to an end, she knew she had to continue to make a living and acting was what she knew she had to do. So, what do you do? You continue to find work, wherever you can!

Bonita's determination to still make money would not be in vain. On September 15, 1941, Bonita signed a contract with RKO. She agreed to appear in three pictures for them within the year. Her salary was a hundred and sixty-six dollars per picture, which was odd, since it wasn't a perfect 200 or 1000 dollars a week. She actually made five films for RKO: *Syncopation* (1942), *Hitler's Children* (1943), *Seven Miles from Alcatraz* (1943), *Youth Runs Wild* (1944) and *The Truth About Murder* (1946).

The issue with RKO was the same as every other studio: What do we do with this woman? What roles do they put her in? Bonita Granville tried to look for good scripts, get roles whenever she could. The roles that she did take, some would say, were not up to her standard. The roles that she took may not have paid her enough, but she made enough to stay afloat during the times of changes. When the roles were becoming more out of her reach, she realized she had to get these parts herself. She had to go out and actually audition, which was new to her, since under the studio system that she was forever apart of, her parts were directly given to her, and if she didn't comply, she would be suspended, but she never had that issue. But now, she was on her own, trying to figure things out. What studio would hire her?

When she ended her time with RKO, she had to do what many actresses had to do: Be a freelancer, meaning, she was not under any contract, she just regularly auditioned for parts, whenever she could. So many of the films that she did, being a freelancer, were tragically B movies, and they weren't enough to be memorable, but in her eyes, she was still making a living. It wasn't her fault, her worst fears were coming to fruition. What was to become of Miss Granville? Was she to rise to prominence again? She was about to learn how she could make her career even better. The best thing about Bonita in this situation and this time period, is that she never ever turned to drugs or drinking. She remained on the rails, rather than failing off it. What she didn't know, is that she was about to experience a whole new addition to her life that would make her a very powerful woman.

All it took, was the entrance of a man, named John Devereaux Wrather Jr. also known as "Jack Wrather."

Bonita smiling for a fan in 1941 (Author's Collection)

Bonita in a publicity for MGM for Thanksgiving (Author's Collection)

Bonita, beginning her timed at RKO (Author's collection

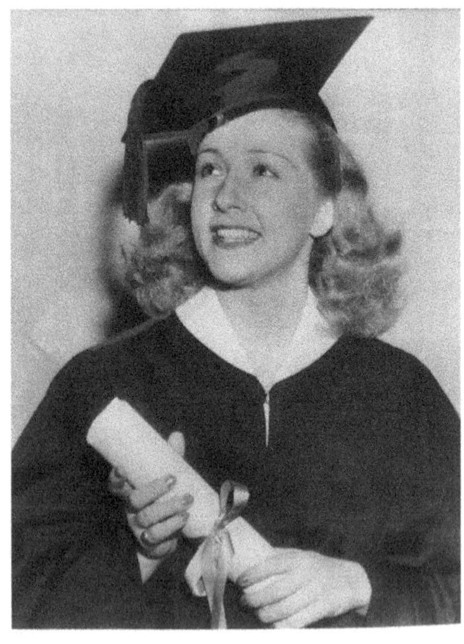

Bonita graduating from high school (Author's Collection)

Bonita in a publicity for fashion (1945) (Author's collection)

Bonita Granville on the set of Andy Hardy Blonde Trouble (1944) : (Gift of Jorge Finkelman)

Bonita in Breakfast in Hollywood *(Author's Personal Collection)*

PHOTO SECTION ONE

Bonita in a Fashion Publicity for MGM (Harry Ransom Center, UT)

Bonita in a Fashion Publicity for MGM (Harry Ransom Center, UT)

Bonita in a Fashion Publicity for MGM (Harry Ransom Center, UT)

Bonita in a Fashion Publicity for MGM (Harry Ransom Center, UT)

Bonita in a Fashion Publicity for MGM (Harry Ransom Center, UT)

Bonita in a Fashion Publicity for MGM (Harry Ransom Center, UT)

Bonita in a Fashion Publicity for MGM (Harry Ransom Center, UT)

Bonita in a Fashion Publicity for MGM (Harry Ransom Center, UT)

Bonita in a Fashion Publicity for MGM (Harry Ransom Center, UT)

Bonita in a Fashion Publicity for MGM (Harry Ransom Center, UT)

Bonita in a Fashion Publicity for MGM (Harry Ransom Center, UT)

Bonita in a Fashion Publicity for MGM (Harry Ransom Center, UT)

Bonita in a Fashion Publicity for MGM (Harry Ransom Center, UT)

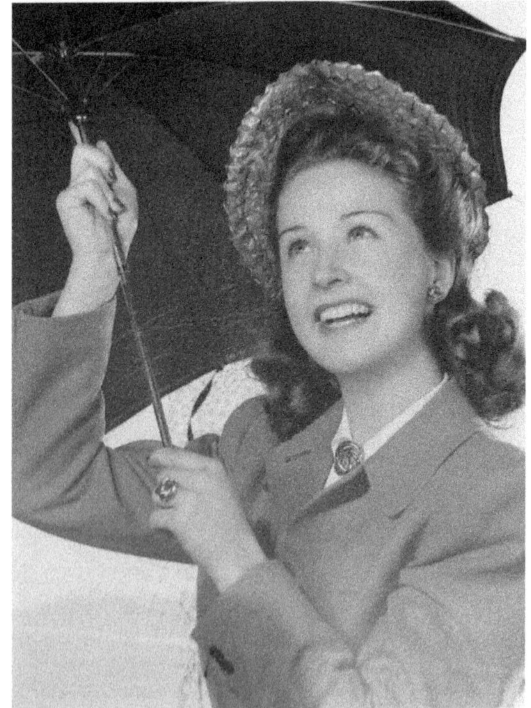

Bonita in a Fashion Publicity for MGM (Harry Ransom Center, UT)

Bonita in a Fashion Publicity for MGM (Harry Ransom Center, UT)

Bonita in a Fashion Publicity for MGM (Harry Ransom Center, UT)

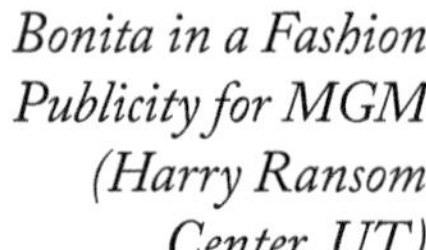

Bonita in a Fashion Publicity for MGM (Harry Ransom Center, UT)

Bonita in a Fashion Publicity for MGM (Harry Ransom Center, UT)

Bonita with her dog, Chin-Chin, 1943 (Harry Ransom Center, UT)

Bonita for MGM, 1943 (Harry Ransom Center, UT)

Bonita for MGM, 1943 (Harry Ransom Center, UT)

Bonita Granville, 1950 (Harry Ransom Center, UT)

PART THREE: MRS. WRATHER

Bonita and Jack, when they first started dating (Author's Collection)

"Time changes, but not love"—Unknown.

Chapter Twelve: Jack Wrather

Jack Wrather is a name that provokes legendary status. He was born John Devereaux Wrather, Jr., on May 24, 1918, in Amarillo, Texas. Jack's life was filled with fun, just as Bonita's had been. In 1939, after receiving his bachelor's degree at the University of Texas, he took on jobs in the oil industry such as pipeline walker, wildcatter and construction supervisor.

In 1940, he took over his father's position in the Wrather Petroleum Company, making it more successful than it already was. During WWII, Wrather served in the Marines until 1945. Believing that the Hollywood entertainment industry was ready for significant expansion after the war, Jack relocated to California. There, he met 24-year-old actress Bonita Granville.

Bonita and Jack's wedding day! (Author's Private Collection)

"It was love at first sight for him, but it was definitely not love at first sight for her"—Gloria Jean.

Chapter Thirteen: "Maybe He Is Mr. Right?"

Mr. Wrather made his appearance in Hollywood in 1947. At this time, Bonita was a freelance actress, getting roles whenever she could. Jack had decided to put his hand in producing. The first project he acquired was *The Guilty*. In *The Guilty*, twin sisters Linda and Estelle (both played by Granville) Mitchell become entangled with two ex-Army roommates Mike Carr and Johnny Dixon. Estelle's insatiable desire for both men lead her to manipulate them against each other, culminating in a murder and the discovery of Linda's body in a barrel on a rooftop. While both men are initial suspects, detective Heller (Regis Toomey) unravels a series of plot twists to uncover the true killer. This low-budget film noir, produced by Jack Wrather, with Bonita Granville starring in a dual role as the twins, mirrors the essences of its genre. The film itself was considered a "B" film, and the budget wasn't much, which didn't help matters. Recognizing Bonita's vulnerability, Jack began to make his move.

As Gloria Jean recalled, when Bonita told her about her first meeting with Jack Wrather,

"She said it wasn't love at first sight. He was a father of two young children, and was newly divorced, which back then was a bit of a red flag [for her]. When I went out to lunch with her one day, we talked about him. I asked if there was anything good about him. Her response? He had money!"

Bonita's superstitions about Jack were uneasy. The man was just divorced. Bonita, being a motherly friend, didn't mind that he had two young children. In fact, she had dreams of becoming a mother, but being a stepmother? She had read in her storybooks that stepmothers could be bad. She was still just a kid herself and she didn't know if she would be a good stepmother. As Gloria Jean also said, "The kids weren't the issue, it was the divorce, that was the issue."

Bonita was considered Catholic, and in some instances, Catholics don't like the idea of divorce. "Bunny's issue with him was that he was newly divorced. She didn't dare ask why, but she thought, if he couldn't make one marriage work, would it work out for me? I told her to go on one date and see if she would even consider going steady with him. She agreed to one date," Gloria Jean recalled in an email in 2015.

Bonita agreed to go on a date with Wrather. When she did, she said she never felt safer in her entire life with a man. The date, as fate would have it, sealed the deal for her. She seemed to have fallen for the Texas oil millionaire. Bonita seemed to take immediately to Jack's two young children.

The press seemed to take to this new romance. Photos of Bunny and Jack going out together seemed to have caused a stir in Hollywood. Bonita wasn't the kind of girl to just get married. She wanted to make sure that the man she married would be with her through thick and thin. When she began dating Mr. Wrather, she noticed that he was really a great businessman, and yet, she felt, they could do great things together.

And great things together they did.

Bonita and Jack's wedding day! (Author's Private Collection)

Jack and Bonita sitting reading a script for The Guilty *(1947): (Author's personal Collection)*

Bonita and Jack, on the Queen Mary II (Gift of Jorge Finkelman)

"Any moment after that, she probably couldn't recall life without him!"—Peggy Moran Koster (1918-2002).

CHAPTER FOURTEEN: "GOOD MORNING, MRS. WRATHER!"

DURING THE TIME of the studio system collapsing, Bonita Granville knew that she had to do something in order to keep her image alive. As she was going steady with Mr. Wrather, he was producing films that she would star in. Jack was getting serious with Bonita. He knew that she was the one for him.

On February 5, 1947, a few days after her twenty-fourth birthday, Bonita Granville became Bonita Granville Wrather. The press capitalized on the newlyweds. "Bonita Granville, one of Hollywood's most eligible bachelor girls, is now married." Bonita's ideal of a real marriage was one that would hopefully last. It was a small ceremony, with Ann Rutherford her matron of honor.

Bonita's wedding was publicized greatly, as she was excited to embark on this new chapter of her life.

Movieland Magazine stated:

> Hollywood's most eligible bachelor girl. She doesn't hesitate to tell you how pleased she is with her new role, for Bonita's never been happier. Her husband is Texas oil millionaire and Monogram producer Jack Wrather. Their "Honeymoon Cottage" is a dream house in Los Angeles' famed Bel Air. Bonita is particularly fond of flowers and plants; so, the grounds are spacious and she tends most of the gardens herself. Her home and her husband have become the most important things in her life; and Hollywood won't be too surprised if Bonita retires from pictures eventually. Mrs. Wrather is a lovely bride whose

> dreams have come true, whose fabulous trousseau, wedding gifts and gleaming new car are understandable reasons why she feels so much like a fairy princess.

In the beginning stages of their marriage, Bonita stayed at home and took care of Wrather's two young children. As Gloria Jean put it, "She had two weeks of that, and basically was bored!"

Bonita, as some had described her, was as jumpy as an energizer bunny. Bonita wanted to be part of the meetings that her husband Jack attended and wanted to be part of the producing side of it. She really wanted to get into the nitty-gritty side of the business. Jack at first was a little against the idea, but Bonita being the fix-it woman she was, he came around and he always was grateful that she took such an interest in his work. Unbeknownst to him, Bonita was always filled with ideas and the ideas that she had could turn into something bigger. In other words, Bonita Granville had the biggest imagination than any male executive. She always creative and that's what made her a wonderful actress. She always knew what worked. The marketing, she had down pat, for she knew what was good and what wasn't. She knew how to please the "audience." With Television coming on the horizon, she really put her marketing skills to work.

One thing that was heading her way would change her life for the better. The way that everything seemed to work in her favor, would change the course of her life, even more so than just being *Nancy Drew.*

Bonita in the 1950s: (Author's Collection)

"All that hair, and all her sweet image, was now a woman who had a good head on her shoulders."

Chapter Fifteen: Cut My Hair

Nineteen fifty, the world of a new era. Babies were being born left and right, the economy was suddenly booming, and now a new kind of entertainment was occurring: Television.

Television was becoming very popular and just like the actors in the silent era, scrambling to see if they'd be perfect for talkies, the golden age actors and actresses were scrambling to see if they could make it on television. A lot of Bonita's contemporaries, such as Deanna Durbin, left Hollywood behind, never to return. Other contemporaries, like Helen Parrish, had a great but brief career on television. Gloria Jean tried to make it on television, but shortly retired from the business completely.

Bonita Granville had another idea in mind, on how to approach this new medium. She began appearing on several TV shows, such as *Climax!* Bonita enjoyed acting in front of the camera, but her sights soon turned to behind the camera.

In 1951, Jack Wrather formed the Wrather TV Production company. He met and formed a production with Maria Helen Alvarez, creating the Wrather-Alvarez broadcasting group.

In 1954, there was a new show being developed about a boy and his collie. The show would be considered one of the longest running shows that ever-graced television. The show was *Lassie*. The show was created by animal trainer Rudd Weatherwax and TV producer Robert Maxwell. From 1957 onward, Jack Wrather, accompanied by Bonita, assumed the roles of producers, making the show an icon it is today. The premise of the series unfolds on a Midwestern farm, spotlighting the heartwarming bond between Lassie and a young farm boy. The narrative shifts its focus to the dog's adventures alongside her forest ranger companions for the next seven years. In the final two years, Lassie finds a new home at a children's sanctuary.

The show had a large cast and even Bonita took part in an episode or two. In the episode "The Wrong Gift," Bonita and her daughter, Linda, both star. In the episode, Timmy gives the wrong gift to his mother (June Lockhart), while Willie (played by Linda), gives her mother (Bonita) the wrong gift. In the episode the life lesson is about understanding and compassion. It was the most impactful episode. Bonita playing "herself" (literally, being a mom and one of the most compassionate women in the world, not to mention the entertainment industry), she was able to show to her true colors, on how being able to listen and have compassion for other people, was incredibly important. Linda remembers being with her mom, and she said it was a wonderful experience and her mom was pro, even though Bonita was more behind the camera, than in front of it.

The series lasted for 19 seasons, making it one of the most successful TV series in history.

When she began her next producing project, *The Lone Ranger*, Bonita, again, took part in some of the episodes, but she remained behind the camera, more than in front of it.

In 1954, the Wrather-Alvarez company made history with another TV show: *The Lone Ranger. The Lone Ranger* was also successful, it lasted for five seasons, unlike *Lassie,* that had 19 seasons.

But nonetheless, The *Lone Ranger* was an immediate success. It was a Western and many people enjoyed that. This was the very start of Television and new ideas were coming into the studios all the time, for new family entertainment. The *Lone Ranger* lasted until 1957.

Bonita Granville understood her job as a producer, but she also had a job to be a mother to Jack's two children. There was also something else on Bunny's mind. She wanted children of her own. Bonita always wanted to be a mom, and yes, she had two loving step-children, but she always wanted some of her very own.

Autographed photo of Bonita (Gift of Laura Jerrolds)

Bunny in her very own sweater (Harry Ransom Center, UT)

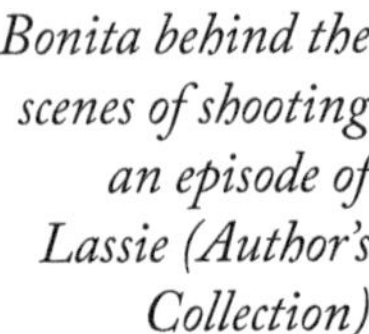

Bonita behind the scenes of shooting an episode of Lassie (Author's Collection)

Bonita with her "fresh new" haircut (Harry Ransom Center, UT)

Linda Wrather and mommy, Bonita- (Gift of Don Ballard)

"One of my greatest joys is being a mother!" Bonita Granville Wrather, 1951

Chapter Sixteen: "Mommy"

Before Bonita began the life of producer and philanthropist, she was first "Mommy" to four children. First, she was a step-mother to Jack's two adoring children, and then on April 7, 1949, her first biological child with Jack was born, a daughter, Linda Bonita Wrather. As Linda said, "Mommy said I love you a lot and we got lots of hugs."

Bonita's journey of motherhood was one that she rather anticipated. She loved being a mother, and, even more so, a grandmother when her children and stepchildren had their own families. In total, Bonita had eleven grandchildren, and let's not get started on how many great-grandchildren she has (spoiler alert, it's more than two!).

Her life as a mother continued around the clock, even as a businesswoman, helping her husband, then being "Mommy." Bonita's role as a mother was huge. In Hollywood, mothers and daughters tend to dislike or downright hate each other. Bonita was lucky enough not to have that kind of relationship with either of her daughters. Bonita loved her kids, and her grandchildren (the ones that she was able to know, a grandson and a granddaughter, both on her daughter's side). She knew that she raised good children and stepchildren.

With some of Bonita's great-grandchildren, it's hard to believe that an actress in the family tree. One of Bonita's grandchildren, seemed to follow in the family footsteps, of being in showbusiness. He is a very successful playwright and has written many award-winning plays. One of Bonita's great-grandchildren, is also trying their hand at acting, almost like Bonita is following through the veins of the family, without them even knowing it. Tragically,

Bonita never got the chance to know a lot of her great-grandchildren, but they are all aware that Bonita Granville Wrather, is in their family, and they really couldn't be prouder.

In the course of Bonita's life, she always knew she wanted a big family. When asked why, she always said, "When I'm gone, who will carry on my name?"

Bonita's daughter really is proud of her, and unlike many mothers in Hollywood, whose daughters have tragic things to say about their moms, and how their moms were "abusive" or "narcissistic," Bonita's daughter said all the opposite things. "So, yes! I knew about Jackie Cooper ....Mom was engaged to him before my dad. I don't think Mom talked about him much so I really don't remember how I know! My mom was a great mom although I had a full time "nanny" that lived with us until I was 13! My parents traveled a lot and my mom worked with my dad after they got married so she was not exactly a "hands on" mom. Lots of the time, my parents took my brother and me traveling with them.... We lived in New York part of the year for several years because my dad had a business there. But whenever we went with them, we always either had our nanny or my maternal grandmother with us... It was a very "Hollywood" childhood but I wouldn't trade it for anyone else's!" My mom said "I love you" a lot and we had plenty of hugs... My mom still acted a little bit after she married my dad. My dad was a movie producer and she acted in his movies and tv shows. Mom gave up acting pretty much to be a wife and a mom. She started helping my dad with his businesses so she was a busy lady for her whole life!"

Bonita was a loving mom, and she really made that lasting impression on her kids. She did everything she could to make it work, and though she did have "help," she still wanted to be the loving mom she always was. There is a saying in Hollywood, "If the daughter doesn't speak well of her mom, that means that she wasn't the best. But if the daughter, speaks highly of her mother, then you know she did everything she could to make her daughter happy." Bonita did just that. She loved her kids and she adored everyone around her. Bonita's daughter, Linda always has spoken highly of her mother and that, is a sign that Bonita did everything she could to make her kids' lives happy and worthwhile. The words "I love you," were always said, and they're even said with Bonita's lineage. Hugs and kisses are so prevalent, and there is love all around, and it shows that Bonita's love for her family, still continues, even today, with the successors of her lineage.

Her daughter, Linda, is one of the sweetest women and she is just like her mother, in every way: Kind, gracious and has a beautiful heart.

Bonita and Linda on the set of Lassie- (Author's Collection)

The birth of Linda Bonita Wrather-(Author's Collection)

Bonita with Linda and her son, Chris (Author's Collection)

Linda and Mommy (Gift of Don Ballard)

Bonita, Linda and Chris (Author's Collection)

Bonita and the man himself, Walt Disney (Author's collection)

"I guess you could say it was a small world after all."

CHAPTER SEVENTEEN: IT'S A SMALL WORLD AFTER ALL!

LIFE COULDN'T BE BETTER for the Wrathers; they were on top of the world, working with top producers, making TV history.

After forming the Wrather-Alvaraze company in 1951, came the biggest success of Wrathers' career: A call from Walt Disney himself.

In the mid-1950s, Disney was trying to capitalize on his success on his first major theme park, Disneyland. He invested so much money that when they came to the hotel aspect, he didn't have any money left. He tried to get some investors, such as the Hilton and Sheraton Hotels, to get involved, but both declined as they stated they had no idea where Anaheim (where the hotel would be built) was. When he approached Jack Wrather, however, things changed. Jack saw an opportunity. Not only as a business, but to network, and gain a whole new meaning of the word businessman. Jack agreed to the project and when he told Bonita about it, she was more than thrilled. "Disney wants us?" She exclaimed. "Yes, darling, and we're gonna do it together!" Jack replied with a kiss.

On March 18, 1955, the ground was broken for the building of the hotel. On October 5 of the same year, the big day arrived! The hotel only had 70 rooms at the time and some of those rooms were for the lobby and offices. Bonita was thrilled to work with the Disney company and, in fact, she had continued to work with the company until the mid-1980s. Bonita filmed a promotional video in the 1970s about all the Disneyland hotel attractions. The woman had three outfit changes, and the guests at the hotel got a glimpse at what fun they could have. She showed at the time, the restaurants, which a lot of them aren't there anymore, the different pavilions, the different attractions, as well the hotel rooms. The hotel rooms were spectacular for the times. It had their own Television set, a rarity for the time as well as balcony for sun tanning. The room seems cozy and spacious.

As Disneyland got larger, the hotel had to be remodeled to accompany those accommodations. The rooms went from 70 to 300. It was the first hotel in Anaheim to offer a room for four people. Shopping and other amenities were added by the late '60s. The hotel looked exquisite, and goodness, no hotel had looked that way since. The hotel came with a large pool, an enclosed patio for people to get sun and a little TV set. What a vacation!

With the hotel booming, behind the scenes life in paradise was crashing and it was crashing, fast. The Wrather and Alvarez company dissolved due to Maria Alvarez marrying her former partner, John Hill, who at the time gave all his shares from his company, to Maria. Jack found out about this and tried to sue John for fraud, tragically that backfired really quickly.

In 1958 however, Wrather took ownership of the production company and the hotel itself. Buy buying all the shares of what was left of the Wrather-Alvarez company. Now, he owned both the hotel and everything with it.

Bonita, of course, did everything she could to make the situation better, but as she said, "Things happen, and sometimes, there's not much we can do." Bonita's involvement with Disney would last up until Jack's death in 1984.

In 2011, Bonita and Jack became Disney Legends, which sounds like a great honor, but Bonita's biography on their website is filled with errors. For example, Bonita was born in New York City, not in Chicago. Also, Jack Wrather was not a Southern California businessman, he was not from California at all, the man was from Texas. However, she is honored with that status, as she should be, A Disney Legend.

The Wrathers in front of the Disneyland Hotel (Gift of Don Ballard)

The Wrathers (Author's Collection)

Bonita and Jack, 1955 (Gift of Dona Ballard)

Bonita and Jack on a Disney ride (Author's Collection)

PHOTO SECTION TWO

Bonita and Linda (Author's Collection)

Bonita Granville on the set of Lassie (Tumblr)

Bonita and Jack Wrather and unidentified guests at the opening of the Disneyland Hotel (Gift of Don Ballard)

Bonita feeling "free" (Author's Collection)

Bonita and Jack, 1956 (Author's Collection)

Bonita, 1980 (Author's Collection)

With Lassie! (Author's Collection)

Bonita in the 1980's (Author's collection)

Bonita out at sea! (Author's Collection)

Bonita and Jack, a few months before his death (Author's collection)

Bonita and an unidentified guest sign the guest book at the opening of the Disneyland Hotel (Author's Collection)

"I got the news that she had passed, Kate—I cried and I cried for days. A woman who did so much for others and who loved bigger than Lucy [Ball]—she was a beacon of light for our world and she was gone. Beauty like hers was rare—and it still is. There hasn't been anyone like her since. No one can top her passion or talent. A woman of love and passion and kindness. I sadly wasn't able to go to the funeral, but I sent my love and support. I am one of the women who were touched by the love of this darling woman. The world lost its light that day and it never really came back"— Gloria Jean.

CHAPTER EIGHTEEN: NOT JUST "A FRIEND OF REAGAN'S"

BONITA'S WORLD was sprouting with various opportunities. She was on the board for many organizations, and various charites, as well as making several public appearances and being a busy woman, she also devoted her time to her husband, Jack, who was still head of the Wrather Corporation.

In the late 1950s, Bonita Granville said goodbye to one of her dearest friends, Helen Parrish, who died from cancer. It was a huge blow for Granville, as Parrish and Granville were dear friends. She also said goodbye to her other dear friend, Judy Garland, in 1969. Bonita realized then that life should not be taken for granted, but she felt other people had.

In the late 70's, Jack hadn't been well, and he was losing his ability to work. Finally, in 1979, Jack went to the doctor and found out something that would devastate his wife; he had cancer. Jack was a heavy smoker, and back then, cigarettes were used by the majority of actors, producers, etc. and there wasn't any "danger" then, but later, people were developing cancer, mainly lung cancer. He managed to live with it and with Bonita, trying to keep the peace, as well, trying to keep her cool, it was not an easy situation.

He managed to live with it for five years and then, tragically, on November 12, 1984, he succumbed to the cancer. Sadly, this left Bonita in a predicament. This meant that she now had to run the company. At the time, Bonita was grieving and she had to put on a brave face. She didn't know how to do it any other way. When her world was crashing, she knew she had to be "brave." She had been that way for a long time. She didn't want to break down, but at the same time, she felt alone. She wanted her partner, her best friend, her lover, and the father of her children. When she went home, she felt the silence a little too much, and when her grandchildren or kids weren't over, she tried to handle grieving the best way she could, by reminiscing the good times, but also the hard times. Marriage, as she knew took a lot of work, give and take, but she wouldn't trade him for all the other men in the world. He worshipped the ground she walked on and she in turn, adored him with stunning admiration. They were perfect for each other and everyone could see that. They were a power couple and they had a marriage that lasted until the day they both died, which in Hollywood, that's rare. Many of her peers were on their fourth divorce, or getting remarried for the fifth time. Not Bonita. She wanted a man, who would stick with her through thick and thin, and with Jack Wrather, that's exactly what she got and now..it was just her, on her own for the first time, in over 30 years.

The way that the press treated Bonita was deplorable. So many went as far to say that she should "pull herself up by her bootstraps," since now she was running the corporation with her son, Chris. She missed Jack. In fact, she needed him. She was independent, and yet she needed him for her support and comfort. Yes, she had her three children (Chris, Linda, and Molly). They were having families of their own, which brought her so much joy, but when they went home, she was left alone with the silence that she was getting used to. For the first time in her life, she felt overwhelmed and unsure of herself.

Not having the man that she had been married to for over two decades was a difficult adjustment. She had to learn to do something she didn't think she'd have to do: live without him. In that span of time, Bonita Granville Wrather became a grandmother (on her daughter Linda's side), she became a philanthropist for many organizations, threw herself into different charitable positions, and was on different company boards, such as the University of Texas (Austin), where her late husband and her son Chris had graduated. She did everything she could to fill her schedule, like she always had. She was continuing on with her life and yet, still grieving for the loss of her husband.

In the fall of 1988, Bonita wasn't feeling well. She went to the doctor and they said she just had a bad cold. Bonita went home, not knowing what was really brewing in her body—she believed them. Instead of getting better, she got worse, severely worse. She went back, and tragically she got news that she didn't think she'd ever get: lung cancer. First and foremost, Bonita hated smoking. She didn't really smoke on her own, but sadly, there was something called social smoking, which basically meant if you went to events, you smoked. Bonita occasionally did smoke, but she really didn't like to.

"Lung cancer, Mrs. Wrather, you have lung cancer." Bonita sat there, trying to process the information. *Lung Cancer. The same thing that she lost her precious Jack to. Now, she is dealing with the same disease.* How long would she last? Would there be options? No. She didn't want them, she wanted to be with her beloved Jack.

Bonita was terrified, and yet, she didn't know what she could really do. In those days, lung cancer, or any form of cancer, was a death sentence.

Bonita knew that she was on borrowed time and checked into Saint John's Medical Center. She was there for only a couple of weeks. When Bonita went to sleep that night on October 10, 1988, she said goodnight to her loved ones and she closed her eyes and went to sleep. She went to sleep for the very last time, and she didn't wake up the next day. On October 11, 1988, Bonita Granville succumbed to her cancer that had been plaguing her body.

Friend and colleague Gloria Jean said this of Bonita's passing when she heard about it on October 12, 1988: "I got the news that she had passed, Kate, I cried and I cried for days. A woman who did so much for others and who loved bigger than Lucy [Ball]—she was a beacon of light for our world and she was gone. Beauty like hers was rare—and it still is. There hasn't been anyone like her since. No one can top her passion or talent. A woman of love and passion and kindness. I sadly wasn't able to go to the funeral, but I sent my love and support. I am one of the women who were touched by the love of this darling woman. The world lost its light that day and it never really came back." The world really did lose its light. The light of a woman who was so gracious and caring, and not to mention a Hollywood legend, that people tended to forget or overlook.

Her obituaries, however, did not reflect that. They took a more "masculine" approach. So many newspapers, including one from the *Roanoke Times*, states "Friend of Reagan's Bonita Wrather dies." Bonita dies, and they make it about Reagan? When Gloria Jean read that headline, her immediate thought was "Are you kidding me?"

It usually was about Reagan, and how she was a "good friend."

"Colleague of Reagan's dies." Is that what Bonita's legacy was burnt down to? Tragically, having headlines such as this, erased all her hard work and her amazing career that she had prior to Reagan ever setting foot in Hollywood. Also, reporters just mentioned that she was "The wife of Jack Wrather." Bonita wasn't just "Mrs. Jack Wrather," she was Bonita Granville for half of her life. She was Bonita Granville, the former child star, turned actress, turned producer, and turned philanthropist. She wasn't anyone's "this or that," she was woman all her own.

Bonita's obituaries didn't make the front page of any newspaper. It wasn't like she was Elizabeth Taylor or anything, who got the front page of every newspaper. The difference between how other major actresses' obituaries got published and Bonita's was like night and day. Bonita only got a fraction of the attention that other stars, such as Mickey Rooney, or Elizabeth Taylor, who engulfed the news circuit when they died, but not Bonita. Half of the newspapers didn't even make her obituary big enough or long enough to even get noticed. Some newspapers, the obituary was so small, you'd miss it and couldn't even find it, which was really disappointing.

Her life was filled with excitement, good times and bad times, but all in all, Bonita Granville would describe her life as lucky, and overall worth it.

"I was an incredibly lucky woman. I had the career that most people would die for, a husband, and a wonderful life. I've been pretty lucky to have been blessed beyond my wildest dreams. If I had to do it all over again, I wouldn't change a thing. I know that people tend to take life for granted, but I don't think I could, not for a moment! Like I said, I was pretty lucky!" She once said in an interview in the early 80's.

Bonita was laid to rest next to her beloved husband at Holy Cross Cemetery in Culver City, California. The funeral was beautiful, a Catholic Mass held in her honor. Family and friends came to pay tribute to their dear Bonita. Her pallbearers were all her grandsons, and that's how she would have wanted it.

Bonita was reunited with her beloved husband and her mother, whom she adored. The thing that really gave actress and friend Gloria Jean peace, as she had a difficult time adjusting to her friend's death, was that she knew that one day she too would be reunited with the sweet blonde who offered her vanilla cake and various special moments of dear friendship. That's the thing about Bonita Granville, no matter what people were going through, she would lend a hand and give her heart and soul to make sure you were okay. It's a quality that many actresses today, really don't have, unless it's put on for publicity. Bonita Granville was just genuinely kind hatred and she knew that there was so much hate in the world and why would to add to that hate? She thought to herself, if the world needs kindness and love, she should be able to give the world just that.

"The world was better with in her it," Gloria Jean recalled in 2017. A lot of fans mourned their favorite star, and the world lost the very first, Nancy Drew. But Bonita Granville proved that she was more than that. She was a STAR. She was Hollywood and she knew how to make Hollywood worth it. Yes, as she said, Hollywood isn't perfect, but in a way, she did what she loved doing: Making people smile. Today, new fans across the globe, of all ages, of all genders and all walks of life, are discovering this pint-size blonde bombshell, who knew how to make the world smile. She really knew how to be comforting, and loving, even when people didn't deserve it. She was the product of the one of the best eras in Hollywood. She worked with some of the biggest names in Hollywood, her resume would blow you away! When she was laid to rest, she knew she was finally reunited with her love, Jack. Bonita's life and legacy continues on, through her family and through her grandchildren, and not to mention the amount of great-grandchildren she has!

Her gravestone reads:

"BONITA GRANVILLE WRATHER
1923 - 1988

BELOVED WIFE, MOTHER, GRANDMOTHER AND FRIEND."

She was indeed all of that, and more. She was a beloved wife, to Jack for over 30 years. She was a beloved mother, to her children and her step children. She was a wonderful grandmother, to the grandchildren she was able to know, and finally she was a very beloved friend, to all who knew her.

Some of her friends, such as Jane Withers, Cora Sue Collins and Gloria Jean, remembered their friend fondly and often, talking about her whenever they could. Though these women have now passed, they never forgot the love and grace that was Bonita Granville. Bonita Granville really brought people together.

"There's nobody like her and there hasn't been anyone like her since. People try to be like her, but they fail. They miss one important detail; she wasn't fake about her kindness and her heart was really as you saw it: good and kind. The thing about Bunny Granville that people will overlook or forget is that she was one of a kind and there will never ever, ever be anyone as good as she was!

Beauty like hers was rare, and it still is!" Gloria Jean stated in an email in 2016. One thing that will always stick out in that email is the ending: "Beauty like hers was rare and still is." Bonita Granville was a rare beauty and yet, as Gloria Jean had said, "There's nobody like her and there hasn't been anyone like her since."

As Gloria Jean said, "The world really lost it's light that day, and it never really came back." Bonita Gloria Granville was now no more, but her legacy continued on, yet it continued on in ways that not everyone knew.

When Nancy Drew is usually spoken about in the media, the first person the reporters mention, is her, because *she was the first one!* In fact, many people have said that her Nancy Drew, was the best out of every adaption of Nancy Drew that has ever been made. Nancy Drew might have been Bonita Granville's most iconic role, but she proved that she was even more than that. She was a gifted actress, and a wonderful philanthropist, who enjoyed charity work and threw herself into other lines work, such as producing and directing as well, as writing a bit.

Unlike some of the stars back in her day, who came out with a "Tell-all book," complaining about how their lives in Hollywood was so horrible, and made mini-series or biopics about their so called "horrific lives," Bonita didn't do any of it, why would she? She had as she described, "Plenty of fun!" She did have fun, she had a ball. Why would she want to write a memoir about her life?

She felt that she didn't need to relive the bad times, or even sometimes, the hard times. They happened and she was grateful for everything. She didn't need to blast anyone for their "wrong doings" or how they "made her feel." Would she have written a stellar autobiography? Yes! Would it have been a bestseller, also yes. But it would be pretty different than most of them. Instead of "complaining" on how her life in Hollywood "sucked," hers would be filled with heartfelt stories and gratitude towards everyone she met. Did she get along with everyone in Hollywood, no, but she was generous and polite, something that today's stars could learn from. She didn't have "feuds" or "long term fights" with anyone, because she felt there was no need to hold on to grudges or to bad blood. That wasn't necessary. There aren't a lot of people who have said bad things about Bonita Granville, and if they did, it's when they were real young and immature and they could laugh about it later. But as an adult, Bonita Granville was revered, admired and above all, respected as a woman in the industry, as a mother and a grandmother and most of all, a friend.

"I miss that woman all the time. I think of her, and I think about her smile and how gracious to me, just starting out in Hollywood," Gloria Jean recalled in 2017. Gloria Jean went on to say this :

"You know when she died, I felt like the world wasn't really the same. People that I knew, started writing books, exploiting and hating each other. I don't think that's what Bunny would have done. She didn't have a mean bone in her body. She was just a fun, loving and not to mention energetic woman. She always told me if you didn't have something nice to say, don't say it all and I live by that. She wasn't bitter about anything or anyone, even Mickey Rooney. She learned that he just had a lot happening to him and we all did, but we weren't all mistreated, and abused like some people say we were. Bonita, wouldn't say that. I think if she were still here, I think she'd be the best mentor to some of these youngsters, who need guidance in this industry. I think Bonita would have aged beautifully and I think that those who got to share the world with her, would have the said the same thing.

The beauty of Bonita Granville, was not just in looks, but in her heart as well. The gracious, kind, fun, and hilarious woman, would have been doing every interview. I think TCM would have had a ball with her. She would have adored everyone there. I think, if TCM was not invented in the early 90's, I think she could have been a regular guest on their programs. Something I feel like people miss these days, is empathy, and Bunny had a lot of it. She never understood why people were hateful, or cruel to each other. Sometimes, I cry about her, and I know why I do. That's how much of a great impact she had on the world and us, the Hollywood child stars of that day. You know when you over someone, even after twenty-years after they're gone, that's when you know they were good people. Bunny, I cry over a lot, especially around her birthday, in February. It sneaks up on me, and it gets me. Sometimes I also cry over when I watch her old films on Television, they play every now and then, usually, it's one of her *Nancy Drew films* and I just start crying. I don't cry in a sad way, I cry because I was lucky to have been apart of her life, as she was of mine. Her beauty, her sweet and gentle nature, I'll never ever forget. It's something you don't really forget. People have forgotten her, but I haven't. She remains, in my constant memory, and I don't want to ever forget her. There are plenty of people in Hollywood that I would love to forget about, but I don't her, because she was that good of a person. God, I know he must have known what he was doing when he created her. He created an angel, and sent it down to Earth and named it *Bonita.* But Bunny Granville was more than just her name, because you know her name means 'beautiful' in Spanish, she was precious, and really quite funny. I don't think people actually knew what a wicked sense of humor she had! My god, she know to make me laugh and everyone else. Her voice, my god, that tone of voice that she had, was always so unique and no one, not even Bacall {Lauren} could have that voice. That woman was born to entertain and she didn't have a stage mother, so to speak, and though she had no father, she was perfectly without him. The most important thing that I do miss about her, is just.. her. I could go on and on about all the wonderful things that I loved about Bunny. I think she was one of the most beautiful and sweetest women in Hollywood."

Bonita Granville was among the good ones, and sadly, has been forgotten over time. The world idolizes Audrey Hepburn, or Elizabeth Taylor, but not Bonita. Why? She was a big star in the 1940's as so was Elizabeth Taylor. But Bonita slowly traded her glitz and glam for something that most of her peers would definitely wished for: A normal and successful life.

Bonita Granville during one of her last public appearences (Author's Collection)

Bonita's final public appearance in 1987 (Author's Collection)

Bonita Granville, and Deanna Durbin at the Hollywood Canteen, 1942. (Author's collection)

"Don't feel sorry for me! I'll get by, I've had plenty of fun!" Bonita Granville.

EPILOGUE: "DON'T FEEL SORRY FOR ME!"

AS THE CROWDS at the Hollywood Canteen began to simmer down, Linda Darnell, Gloria Jean, Deanna Durbin, Bonita Granville, Anne Shirley and Joan Leslie were all standing around talking. Gloria Jean recalled that night: "The girls were all talking about what would become of them in 10 years. Who would feel sorry for us? I recall Bunny looking at us and rolling her eyes. She said plainly, "I don't want anyone feeling sorry for me! I've gotten by and I've had plenty of fun!" Bunny walked to the door and when she opened the canteen door, the light shone on her so brightly, she looked like an angel that was walking into Heaven. She looked like she was about to conquer the world!"

Bonita Granville did just that. She didn't let the world feel sorry for her. She did conquer the world of entertainment and she became a legend. This woman did so much for the world while she was still on Earth and, even today, after 36 years of being gone, her impact is still felt. In 2023, Bonita would have celebrated 100 years of her birth. Sadly, she didn't get to see it on Earth, but it was felt by thousands of movie lovers all over the world. In time, the world would learn to grieve her, and so many of her peers who would precede her in death. Helen Parrish in 1959, Linda Darnell in 1965, Judy Garland in 1969, and then so many went after her. Her best friend and bridesmaid, Ann Rutherford, died in 2012, Deanna Durbin in 2013, Joan Leslie in 2015, Gloria Jean in 2018, Jane Withers in 2024, and the last of them, Cora Sue Collins, in 2025.

As Bonita's legacy continues to be discovered by new fans over the world and still appreciated by those who knew her or of her, the radiant beauty's kindness would always be a treasure. The people that usually discover her, find *Nancy Drew* first, which is her most iconic role. When the new fan discovers her other amazing work, they end up looking her up on IMBD and finally getting to watch her. It makes a lot of her family smile when they realize that Bonita Granville is still relevant to the world.

In 2019, in the *New York Times,* Bonita Granville was spoken about.

In that, we should give our thanks to this larger-than-life wonder woman who gave love and support to everyone and, yet, taught us the biggest life lesson: "It's not about how much money you've made that makes you a successful person, it's the amount of love you give that will define your success"—Bonita Granville, 1943.

In loving memory of:

Bonita Gloria Granville Wrather (1923-1988), who saved lives and brought so many together.

The happy Bunny in 1960: (Author's Collection)

TIME WILL SHARE HER: A NOTE ABOUT THE AUTHOR

IN 2004, a young girl was visiting her grandparents in Fort Worth. The girl was watching a movie with her granny. That movie was *Nancy Drew... Reporter*. Her granny pointed out, "Look at the blonde!" The girl looked at the sweet blonde girl, and the girl was already attached. That girl, who was at the time 12, was me. Hi! I'm Kate Arndt (née Gaddis), and I have loved Bonita Granville Wrather since I was in the 5th grade. I loved her so much that I wouldn't let her go and she wouldn't let me go either. I first watched all her Nancy Drew films and then I proceeded to view other movies. I had always wondered why this woman hadn't been written about or why she didn't publish her own memoir.

Fast forward to 11 years later (2015), when I encountered an actress who would be my only window at that time, to Bonita Granville, Gloria Jean. Gloria Jean had opened the floodgates to all the stories of Bunny and that world of old Hollywood. Through Gloria Jean I was able to ask my questions and, over a few years, I was able to know who Bunny was.

In 2023, many of my peers, aware of my deep admiration for Bunny Granville, urged me to write about her. In July of that year, I called her daughter, and asked her permission to do it. She was, of course, delighted, and thus, I began this journey of writing about the woman who got swept under the rug all the time, to the point of where TCM doesn't even show her films except maybe once in a blue moon. A woman who Disney fans don't even know brought to life the Disneyland hotel and yet, she was still swept under the rug. I was devastated by this. I was also upset by the fact that no one had even bothered to write a book about her, except put her in sections of books that only mention her as Nancy Drew. That wasn't enough for me. I wanted to know more about this incredible woman who did so much than I can even imagine. A woman who shook hands with legendary figures such as the Beatles, and knew Debbie Reynolds and even ate dinners with dignitaries beyond my comprehension.

In August of 2023, I began my biography journey with a visit to the Harry Ransom Center, a part of the University of Texas in Austin, Texas. They had recently gotten all of Bonita's memorabilia and I was the first one to check it all out! I was so astonished and not to mention overwhelmed by so much Granville information. This woman, who I had loved for so long, was now finally getting her time to shine! While so many people are writing biographies on stars such as Mickey Rooney or Elizabeth Taylor, I wanted to write about a woman whom not many people were aware of.

"If you knew Bonita personally, you called her Bunny. No one ever really called her Bonita," Gloria Jean told me on a phone call in 2015. You're probably wondering, "How did Gloria Jean know Bunny so well?" To answer this, a lot of the child stars in the 1930s-1940s all ran in the same circles, meaning that they would see each other at parties, or at different events, or even got the chance to know each other, or worked with another. "I never got the chance to work with Bunny, but I knew her up until her marriage to Jack," Gloria Jean said.

With the help of Lantern, I got the chance to see Bonita Granville in Hollywood magazines from that era. People have told me she wasn't a big star! Yes, she was, but she decided that instead of going off the rails like some of her peers did, she wanted to do something better with her life: Do the business side of Hollywood. Plus, she married a wonderful man, who gave her everything she could ever want: A loving home and a beautiful family, which she always wanted, and now, she has a legacy that she couldn't even comprehend. I'll admit, writing this has not been easy, due to seeing so much about how she was treated by other people, which made me upset and angry, because how could they do that to such a wonderful person? Bonita, I know, had her faults, but as Gloria Jean always said, "Nobody's perfect, but Bonita Granville was pretty damn close!"

With Bonita being an underrated figure of Hollywood, I thought she was a perfect subject to research. When I began this journey a few years ago, I had tried to gather a lot of my sources and my research items and then, I got the green light on the biography from the family (her daughter's side, that is!) and I got straight to work. As much as I love Bonita Granville, and I adore her to bits and pieces, I did have to think like a biographer and a writer, where I had to cover the good, the bad and sometimes the downright sad/ugly. But, with Bonita Granville Wrather, I hope that you have fallen in love with her as much as I have.

Also, as an autistic woman, I have found Bonita to be very comforting, as she understood the emotions I felt. Let me explain this a bit better. As an autistic woman, I find it hard to express my emotions and feelings. Yet, when I watch her, I am able to understand how to express my feelings and emotions. To me, Bonita Granville is more than just a woman that I have watched and admired my whole life, she's become really apart of who I am. This woman, when I began my journey to write about her, I will admit, I was nervous, because I have read biographies before, and I know how some people focus on one particular part of their lives and make them look like horrendous people, or I've also read biographies where they were just "high and dry" basic information, about how much money they made, etc. Not me, I wanted the personal stories, the stories that no one knew about. Thanks to a few actresses I was able to speak to, Cora Sue Collins, Ann Blyth and finally, Gloria Jean, I was able to get those said stories. I wanted to get the nitty gritty, because that's just me.

With Bonita Granville, I wanted to share the side of her that no one would ever see. I wanted to see what I could find, besides, *She was just Nancy Drew* and all. But I wanted to tell stories from the people who knew her when she was alive. I didn't get the chance to share the Earth with Bonita Granville Wrather. She died in 1988; I was born in 1992. So just a few years off.

In 2019, I was fortunate enough to reach out to Bunny's daughter who graciously replied and we began a friendship. We had begun corresponding mainly through text, and a few phones calls here and there. Her daughter, Linda, became a fast friend and one of my favorite contacts I have ever reached out to. I made a promise to Bonita, that if her daughter and I became friends, I would do everything I could to take care of her, and that is a promise that I intended to keep. In 2022, after I got married, her daughter and I arranged to meet. Not only did I meet her daughter, I met her granddaughter (her daughter's daughter!) for the first time. It was such a beautiful moment and it was a moment I would never forget it. In 2024, I was able to see Bonita's family again, this time, I got to meet the great grandchildren! It was wonderful and even more emotional for me.

When I got to sit down and talk with Bonita's daughter, we got to share our love for her mom and her work.

When I look at Bonita Granville, I know she's so underrated and she's different than most people I grew up watching. She's one of my personal favorites. Her, Deanna Durbin and Gloria Jean, are my favorites and I know that all three of them, don't really have biographies, with the exception of Gloria Jean, who wrote her autobiography with a married couple.

Bonita is unique and it's no wonder why I fell in love with her in 5th grade. She was a comfort to me when I was feeling alone and she still does. Do you ever miss people that you feel connected to? I do. At times, I cry cause I miss her so much and I know that sounds weird to the average person, but that's how it feels, I just feel like she's been there for me, and she has, in ways that are hard to describe.

"Time will share her," Is a quote I've heard from an old friend of mine. Meaning, that even though she's gone, time, will not pass for her, and she will.

As for my thanks, I extend it to Jorge Finkelman for the photos and encouragement. Laura Jerrods, Emily Evans, Addy Navarro, Michael Holland, and countless others (you all know who you are!): I love you all so much!

My sweet pharmacists, Heidi and Kelly, thank you for believing in me to continue to write about Bonita.

To my late grandmothers, who taught me that Bonita Granville is there to help me and she always will be.

To Gloria Jean Cellini, my beautiful friend, how I miss you and thank you for sharing your life with me.

To my wonderful in-laws, Karen and Larry Arndt, thank you for loving me and fueling my love of Bunny.

To my darling husband, Kevin, my whole world, and whom, I am so ever grateful for. I can't wait to watch more Bunny films with you!

For Linda, you are my whole world. You and your mother mean so much to me. Thanks for taking a chance on me, and becoming one of my best friends. I love you with all my heart.

To Sabrina and the kids: Bun Bun always loves you and she still will. Love you all so much!

To Bonita Gloria Granville (Wrather): You came into my life at a time when I needed somcone to let me know I'd be okay, and you still want to make sure that I'm okay. I love you and I always will.

To everyone else involved with this book, thank you for your support and love!

Kate

The Icon, the Legend, Bonita Granville : Author's Collecton

THE STAR! Filmography

Westward Passage (1932): Little Olivia
Cavalcade (1933): Fanny [age 7]
Cradle Song (1933): Carmen
The Life of Vergie Winters (1934): Joan Shadwell, as a child
A Wicked Woman (1934): Girl on train
Ah, Wilderness! (1935): Mildred
These Three (1936): Mary Tilford
The Garden of Allah (1936): Child in convent
Song of the Saddle (1936): Little Jen
Call It a Day (1937): Ann Hilton
It's Love I'm After (1937): Gracie Kane
Maid of Salem (1937): Virginia
Quality Street (1937): Isabella
The Plough and the Stars (1937): Mollser
The Life of Emile Zola (1937): Violet
My Bill (1938): Gwen Colbrook
Hard to Get (1938): Connie
White Banners (1938): Sally Ward
The Beloved Brat (1938): Roberta
Nancy Drew: Detective (1938): Nancy Drew
The Angels Wash Their Faces (1939): Peggy Finnegan
Nancy Drew... Trouble Shooter (1939): Nancy Drew
Nancy Drew and the Hidden Staircase (1939): Nancy Drew
Nancy Drew... Reporter (1939): Nancy Drew
Third Finger, Left Hand (1940): Vicky Sherwood
Gallant Sons (1940): Kate Pendleton
Those Were the Days! (1940): Martha Scroggs
The Mortal Storm (1940): Elsa
Escape (1940): Ursula
Forty Little Mothers (1940): Doris
*The Wild Man of Borne*o (1941): Francine
H. M. Pulham, Esq. (1941): Mary Pulham
The People vs. Dr. Kildare (1941): Frances Marlowe
Down in San Diego (1941): Betty Haines
Syncopation (1942): Kit Latimer
Now, Voyager (1942): June Vale

The Glass Key (1942): Opal Madvig
Hitler's Children (1943): Anna Muller
Seven Miles from Alcatraz (1943): Anne Porter
Youth Runs Wild (1944): Toddy
Song of the Open Road (1944): Bonnie
Andy Hardy's Blonde Trouble (1944): Kay Wilson
Senorita from the West (1945): Jeannie Blake
The Beautiful Cheat (1945): Alice
Breakfast in Hollywood (1946): Dorothy Larsen
Suspense (1946): Ronnie
The Truth About Murder (1946): Christine Allen
The Guilty (1947): Linda Mitchell/Estelle Mitchell
Love Laughs at Andy Hardy (1947): Kay Wilson
Strike It Rich (1948): Julie Brady
Guilty of Treason (1950): Stephanie Varna
The Lone Ranger (1956): Welcome Kilgore

Television Appearances:

1951:
Armstrong Circle Theatre, "That's Simon's Girl"
The Bigelow Theatre, "Make Your Bed"
Somerset Maugham TV Theatre, "Masquerade"
Lux Video Theatre, "Not Guilty - of Much"
Gruen Guild Playhouse, "Hit and Run" and "One Strange Day"

1952:
The Schaefer Century Theatre, "I Saw It Happen"
Chevron Theatre, "Yesterday's World" and "Annual Honeymoon"
The Unexpected, "The Woman Who Left Herself"

1953:
Broadway Television Theatre, "Guest in the House"
The Ford Television Theatre, "The Son-in-Law"

1955:
Crown Theatre with Gloria Swanson, "The Antique Shop"
The Eddie Cantor Comedy Theatre, "The Suspicious Husband"

Schlitz Playhouse of Stars, "Sentence to Death"
Climax!, "The Healer"

1956:
Ethel Barrymore Theatre, "Lady Investigator"
Matinee Theater, "The 25th Hour"
This is the Life, "Burden Made Light"
Climax!, "The Fifth Wheel"

1957:
Lux Video Theatre, "One Way Passenge" and "Stand-In for Murder"
Science Fiction Theatre, "Killer Tree"
The United States Steel Hour, "Shadow in the Sky"

1958:
Studio One, "The Fair-Haired Boy"
Target, "Edge of Terror"

1959:
Playhouse 90, "The Velvet Alley"

1960:
Lassie, "The Wrong Gift"

1961:
The Best of the Post, "The Valley of the Blue Mountain"

1963-1972:
Lassie, Narrator

1965:
Lassie, "Lassie's Teamwork"

1966:
Lassie, "Lassie the Voyager: Part 3"

1968:
Lassie, "Hanford's Point: Part 3"

Producer:
Lassie, 1959-1973, 374 episodes

1963:
Lassie's Great Adventure
Lassie: A Christmas Tail

1967:
Flight of the Cougar (TV Movie)

1968:
Lassie: The Adventures of Neeka (TV Movie)

1970:
Lassie: Well of Love (TV Movie)

1978:
The Magic of Lassie

Radio Appearances

1943:
It's Time to Smile
The Lux Radio Theatre, "Hitler's Children"

1944:
The Radio Hall of Fame
It's Time to Smile
G.I. Journal

1945:
Suspense, "Bank Holiday"
G.I. Journal

1946:
The Continental Celebrity Club
The Bill Stern Colgate Sports Newsreel
Show Stoppers

1948:
Studio One, "Wednesday's Child"
Hollywood's Open House
Guest Star

1950:
Obsession, "Cousin Charlie"

1951:
Stars On Parade, "An April Issue"

1952:
Family Theater, "The Promise"
Stars Over Hollywood, "Three's a Family"
Stars Over Hollywood, "Nocturne In Black and White"

1953:
Family Theatre, "Eclipse"

1959:
Memoirs of the Movies, "The Film Factories"

No Dates:
Words With Music
Proudly We Hail, "Charity Ball"

Works Cited

"Access Newspaper Archive Institutional Version | Unauthorized User." Newspaperarchive.com, 2024, access.newspaperarchive.com/us/california/long-beach/independent-press-telegram/1972/07-30/page-91. Accessed 3 Dec. 2024.

Bros, Warner. "Nancy Drew and the Hidden Staircase (Warner Bros. Pressbook, 1939) - Lantern." Mediahist.org, 2024, lantern.mediahist.org/catalog/pressbook-wb-nancy-drew-and-the-hidden-staircase_0004. Accessed 4 Dec. 2024.

---. "Nancy Drew Reporter(Warner Bros. Pressbook, 1939) - Lantern." Mediahist.org, 2022, lantern.mediahist.org/catalog/pressbook-wb-nancy-drew-reporter_0003. Accessed 4 Dec. 2024.

---. "Nancy Drew Reporter(Warner Bros. Pressbook, 1939) - Lantern." Mediahist.org, 2022, lantern.mediahist.org/catalog/pressbook-wb-nancy-drew-reporter_0008. Accessed 4 Dec. 2024.

---. "Nancy Drew Reporter(Warner Bros. Pressbook, 1939) - Lantern." Mediahist.org, 2022, lantern.mediahist.org/catalog/pressbook-wb-nancy-drew-reporter_0007. Accessed 4 Dec. 2024.

---. "Nancy Drew Trouble Shooter(Warner Bros. Pressbook, 1939) - Lantern." Mediahist.org, 2022, lantern.mediahist.org/catalog/pressbook-wb-nancy-drew-trouble-shooter_0009. Accessed 4 Dec. 2024.

Cellini, Gloria Jean . Gloria Jean . 15 Apr. 2015.

Had multiple Interviews with her in 2016, 2017, and finally in 2018. Phone Interviews and emails .

Co, Spanish-American Pub. "Cinelandia (May 1942) - Lantern." Mediahist.org, 2023, lantern.mediahist.org/catalog/cinelandia-1942-05_0011. Accessed 4 Dec. 2024.

---. "Cinelandia (May 1942) - Lantern." Mediahist.org, 2023, lantern.mediahist.org/catalog/cinelandia-1942-05_0008. Accessed 4 Dec. 2024.

Company, Chalmers Publishing. "Cine-Mundial (1944) - Lantern." Mediahist.org, 2024, lantern.mediahist.org/catalog/cinemundial29unse_0398. Accessed 4 Dec. 2024.

Company, Dell Publishing. "Modern Screen (Dec 1937 - Nov 1938) - Lantern." Mediahist.org, 2024, lantern.mediahist.org/catalog/modernscreen1617unse_1271. Accessed 4 Dec. 2024.

Cooper, Jackie, and Richard Kleiner. Please Don't Shoot My Dog : The Autobiography of Jackie Cooper. New York, Berkley, 1982, pp. 129–135, 171.

Donald Ballard. "Vintage 1970s Disneyland Hotel Channel 6 In-Room Guest Services Footage." YouTube, 27 Feb. 2023, www.youtube.com/watch?v=oW84P4OWRVw&list=PL90ReqZlW4MKpPG6YbuVsR7X9y4shz1xH&index=2. Accessed 4 June 2024.

Endless Wars. "Celebrities and Civilians Volunteer at the Hollywood Canteen." YouTube, 1 Dec. 2015, www.youtube.com/watch?v=jygpcTb_17Y&list=PL90ReqZlW4MKpPG6YbuVsR7X9y4shz1xH&index=1. Accessed 4 Nov. 2024.

Fawcett Publications, Inc. "Hollywood (1941) - Lantern." Mediahist.org, 2024, lantern.mediahist.org/catalog/hollywood30fawc_0176. Accessed 4 Dec. 2024.

Finocchario, Linda Wrather. Interview Wth Linda Bonita Wrather Finocchario . Jan. 2019.

I first met Linda in 2019 and have been friends with her ever since .

Group, Macfadden. "Movieland. (Vol. 3, Feb. 1945-Jan. 1946) - Lantern." Mediahist.org, 2022, lantern.mediahist.org/catalog/movielandtvtimev03unse_0427. Accessed 4 May 2024.

---. "Movieland. (Vol. 6, Feb. 1948-Jan. 1949) - Lantern." Mediahist.org, 2022, lantern.mediahist.org/catalog/movielandtvtimev06unse_1009. Accessed 4 Dec. 2024.

Magazine, Photoplay. "Photoplay (Jan - Jun 1941) - Lantern." Mediahist.org, 2024, lantern.mediahist.org/catalog/photoplay118phot_0254. Accessed 4 Dec. 2024.

---. "Photoplay (Jul - Dec 1940) - Lantern." Mediahist.org, 2024, lantern.mediahist.org/catalog/photoplay52chic_0146.

Magazine, Screenland. "Screenland (Jul–Dec 1946) - Lantern." Mediahist.org, 2024, lantern.mediahist.org/catalog/screenland5025unse_0328. Accessed 10 Oct. 2024.

---. "Screenland (May 1943-Oct 1944) - Lantern." Mediahist.org, 2024, lantern.mediahist.org/catalog/screenland4748unse_0014. Accessed 4 Dec. 2024.

Media. "Modern Screen - Lantern." Mediahist.org, 2024, lantern.mediahist.org/catalog/modernscreen26unse_0588. Accessed 4 May 2023.

Newspaper Archive. "Access Newspaper Archive Institutional Version | Unauthorized User." Newspaperarchive.com, 2024, access.newspaperarchive.com/us/pennsylvania/bristol/bristol-bucks-county-courier/1966/06-18/page-35. Accessed 4 July 2024.

---. "Access Newspaper Archive Institutional Version | Unauthorized User." Newspaperarchive.com, 2024, access.newspaperarchive.com/us/wisconsin/kenosha/kenosha-news/1982/02-24/page-28. Accessed 4 Sept. 2024.

---. "Access Newspaper Archive Institutional Version | Unauthorized User." Newspaperarchive.com, 2024, access.newspaperarchive.com/us/ohio/dover/dover-daily-reporter/1960/09-24/page-17. Accessed 4 Nov. 2024.

---. "Access Newspaper Archive Institutional Version | Unauthorized User." Newspaperarchive.com, 1960, access.newspaperarchive.com/us/ohio/dover/dover-daily-reporter/1960/09-24/page-17. Accessed 4 Dec. 2024.

---. "Access Newspaper Archive Institutional Version | Unauthorized User." Newspaperarchive.com, 1968, access.newspaperarchive.com/us/pennsylvania/gettysburg/gettysburg-times/1968/11-02/page-11. Accessed 4 Dec. 2024.

Street. "Picture Play Magazine (1937) - Lantern." Mediahist.org, 2024, lantern.mediahist.org/catalog/pictureplay4547stre_1145. Accessed 9 June 2024.

TheMagicalHotel. "1956 Disneyland Hotel Grand Opening Rare Footage & Images." YouTube, 15 Feb. 2012, www.youtube.com/watch?v=TfwyutwjBQI. Accessed 4 Dec. 2023.

Wrather, Bonita Granville. Bonita Granville Wrather Interview. June 1959.

---. Letters from Bonita .

Bonita Granville wrote letters to her friends and Jackie Cooper- found at the Harry Rasom Room .

Yesterworld Entertainment. "The Rise & Fall of the Original Disneyland Hotel." YouTube, 30 Jan. 2020, www.youtube.com/watch?v=rctkG-VUbDc&list=PL90ReqZlW4MKpPG6YbuVsR7X9y4shz1xH&index=10. Accessed 4 Oct. 2024.

www.ingramcontent.com/pod-product-compliance
Ingram Content Group UK Ltd.
Pitfield, Milton Keynes, MK11 3LW, UK
UKHW021906190726
13853UKWH00002B/535